IRGUN
REVISIONIST ZIONISM 1931–1948

GERRY VAN TONDER

Pen & Sword
MILITARY

To my son Andries

The Irgun emblem.

First published in Great Britain in 2019 by
PEN AND SWORD MILITARY
an imprint of
Pen and Sword Books Ltd
47 Church Street
Barnsley
South Yorkshire S70 2AS

Copyright © Gerry van Tonder, 2019

ISBN 978 1 52672 869 2

The right of Gerry van Tonder to be identified as the author of this work
has been asserted in accordance with the Copyright, Designs and Patents Act 1988.

A CIP record for this book is available from the British Library All rights reserved.
No part of this book may be reproduced or transmitted in any form or by any means, electronic or
mechanical including photocopying, recording or by any information storage and retrieval system,
without permission from the Publisher in writing.

Every reasonable effort has been made to trace copyright holders of material reproduced in this book,
but if any have been inadvertently overlooked the publishers will be pleased to hear from them.

Typeset by Aura Technology and Software Services, India
Printed and bound by TJ International Ltd, Padstow, Cornwall

Pen & Sword Books Ltd incorporates the imprints of Pen & Sword
Archaeology, Atlas, Aviation, Battleground, Discovery, Family History, History, Maritime, Military,
Naval, Politics, Railways, Select, Social History, Transport, True Crime, Claymore Press, Frontline
Books, Leo Cooper, Praetorian Press, Remember When, Seaforth Publishing and Wharncliffe.

For a complete list of Pen and Sword titles please contact
Pen and Sword Books Limited
47 Church Street, Barnsley, South Yorkshire, S70 2AS, England
email: enquiries@pen-and-sword.co.uk
website: www.pen-and-sword.co.uk

CONTENTS

Timeline	5
Introduction	11
1. Custodians of Zion	14
2. The Hebrew Soldier	31
3. Truce and Revolt	63
4. Smite the Enemy Hard	81
5. An Eye for an Eye	96
6. Arms Not Votes	113
Sources	124
Index	125

Irgun Anthem

Tagar –
Through all obstacles and enemies
Whether you go up or down
In the flames of revolt
Carry a flame to kindle—never mind!
For silence is filth
Worthless is blood and soul
For the sake of the hidden glory
To die or to conquer the hill –
Yodefet, Masada, Betar

TIMELINE

1517
Four centuries of Turkish rule over Palestine commence.

1840
15 July: The Convention of London is signed between the United Kingdom, Austria, Prussia and Russia on the one hand and the Ottoman Empire on the other, offering Khedive Mohammed Ali the Sanjak (prefecture) of Acre, in what is now Israel.

1896
14 February: Theodor Herzl, considered to be the founder of modern Zionism and the father of the modern state of Israel, releases *Der Judenstaat*, a publication advocating a Jewish homeland.

1897
29–31 August: The inaugural congress of the Zionist Organization is held at Basel, Switzerland.

1904
July: Upon the death of Theodor Herzl, a Ukrainian-born Jew, Ze'ev (born Vladimir) Jabotinsky assumes leadership of the right-wing Zionists.

1905
In Russia, Ze'ev Jabotinsky calls on Europe's Jews to consolidate and demand autonomous rights for minority ethnic groups.

1908
On behalf of the World Zionist Organisation, Ze'ev Jabotinsky takes up the position of editor-in-chief of the Turkish daily newspaper *Jeune Turc* in Constantinople.

1915
Russian-born Jew and Zionist activist Joseph Trumpeldor forms the 650-strong volunteer Zion Mule Corps within the British Army, with the objective of helping the British wrest Palestine from the Ottoman Empire.

1916

26 May: After participating in the Gallipoli campaign, the Zion Mule Corps is disbanded.

Ze'ev Jabotinsky, Theodor Trumpeldor and 120 former members of the Zion Mule Corps join 16 Platoon, 20th Battalion, London Regiment.

1917

August: The British Army formally raises five battalions of Jewish volunteers, designated the 38th–42nd (Service Battalions), Royal Fusiliers, and unofficially referred to as the Jewish Legion.

2 November: British Foreign Secretary Arthur Balfour, in a letter to Lord Rothschild, declares his country's sympathy with Zionist aspirations, adding that the government is in favour of an independent Jewish state in Palestine.

9 December: Jerusalem surrenders to British general, Edmund Allenby.

28 December: Colonel Ronald Storrs is appointed military governor of Jerusalem.

1920

1 March: Yosef Trumpeldor and five other Jews are shot and killed in a shootout between Jewish settlers and several hundred Arabs at Tel Hai.

4–7 April: Palestinian Arabs riot against Jews in Jerusalem's Old City during the Muslim festival of Nebi Musa, the name of what is believed to be the tomb of Moses on the West Bank.

1921

1–7 May: Starting off as a fight between two rival Jewish groups, Arabs commence a series of attacks against Jews in widespread disorder known as the Jaffa Riots. Ninety-five Arabs and Jews are left dead.

1925

April: The Union of Revisionist Zionists, *Brit HaTzionim HaRevizionistim* (*HaTzohar*), is founded in Paris under the leadership of Ze'ev Jabotinsky.

October: Much-lauded Field Marshal Herbert Plumer, Baron Plumer, becomes High Commissioner of the British Mandate for Palestine.

1926

June: The eighteen-year-old Yefim Gordin—later Chaim 'Shalom' Halevi—arrives in Haifa from Vilna (Vilnius), Lithuania.

Timeline

1927

11 July: A 6.3-magnitude earthquake kills hundreds and badly damages thousands of buildings throughout mandatory Palestine and Trans-Jordan, including the cities of Jerusalem, Jericho, Ramle, Tiberias and Nablus.

1928

23 September: In Jerusalem, on the morning of the Jewish holy festival Yom Kippur, British constable Douglas Duff and ten armed policemen forcibly remove elderly Jewish worshippers and a screen they are using to segregate the sexes at the sacred Western Wall.

November: Sir John Chancellor succeeds Plumer as High Commissioner of the British Mandate.

1929

23–29 August: In the Buraq Uprising, also known as the 1929 Massacres, Arabs murder 133 Jews in various centres during riots over access to Jerusalem's Western Wall.

1931

April: The *Irgun Zvai Leumi*—National Military Organization—is founded to fight for 'national freedom and independence'.

1933

16 June: Prominent Jewish politician and proponent of Arab dialogue, thirty-four-year-old Dr Chaim Arlosoroff is assassinated in Tel Aviv by Revisionist Zionists.

October: Palestinian Arabs demonstrate against the mandate's Jewish immigration policy, clashing with British police in Jerusalem, Nablus, Haifa and Jaffa.

1936–1939

In what became known as the Great Revolt, Palestinian Arabs rise up against the British mandatory administration. An estimated 5,000 Arabs, 262 British Army personnel and 300 Jews are killed.

1937

11–14 November: The Irgun conducts its first terror attacks on Arab targets throughout Palestine.

1938

28 March: Arabs kill six Jews in a vehicle ambush on the Acre–Safad road.

21 April: Operatives from Revisionist Zionist youth movement Betar unsuccessfully carry out an attack on an Arab bus on the Tiberias–Rosh Pina road.

29 June: Shlomo Ben-Yosef, convicted of carrying arms of war on 21 April, is hanged at the British-run Acre Prison, becoming a martyr for the Revisionists.

6 July: A Zionist activist bomb in a Haifa market kills twenty-one Arabs.

25 July: A second bomb in a Haifa market kills thirty-nine Arabs.

26 August: A further bomb explodes in Jaffa's vegetable market, killing twenty-four Arabs.

1940

August: The Revisionist Zionist organization *Lohamei Herut Israel*, Lehi—Fighters for the Freedom of Israel—under Avraham Stern is formed to force the British out of Palestine.

1941

20 May: Founder member and commander-in-chief of the Irgun, David Raziel, is killed in Iraq when the car he is travelling in is bombed by a German aircraft.

1942

12 February: Former Irgun leader and founder of the breakaway militant organization, Lehi, Avraham Stern, while fleeing from the British authorities is shot dead by British detectives in Tel Aviv.

1944

1 February: Irgun leader and future Israeli prime minister Menachem Begin issues his 'freedom or death' revolt proclamation.

12 February: Elements of the Irgun detonate a bomb in the Immigration Department building in Tel Aviv.

27 February: The Irgun bomb the Income Tax offices in Tel Aviv, Jerusalem and Haifa.

23 March: Three British constables are fatally injured when an Irgun bomb explodes at the CID station in Haifa.

24 March: In a shootout after a failed Irgun attempt to detonate a bomb at the CID headquarters in Jerusalem, an Irgun fighter and a British inspector die.

27 March: British authorities impose a curfew in Jerusalem, Tel Aviv and Haifa.

17 May: The Irgun conduct a successful attack on the central radio broadcasting station at Ramele.

14 July: The Land Registry Office in Jerusalem is razed and two Arab constables killed.

15 July: Irgun fighters capture a British explosives truck, killing a British constable.

August: The Irgun sets up its own printing press to produce Revisionist propaganda.

23 August: The Irgun carry out arms raids at CID barracks in Jaffa, Neve Shaanan and Abu-Kabir.

September: The British war cabinet authorizes the raising of the Jewish Infantry Brigade Group.

27 September: Dubbed the 'Day of the Shofar', the Irgun attacks British police Tegart forts at Haifa, Beit Dragon near Jerusalem, Katra and Qalgilya.

6 November: British minister of state in the Middle East, Walter Edward Guinness, 1st Baron Moyne, is assassinated in Cairo by Lehi fighters.

1945

27 December: The Irgun and Lehi attacks on CID headquarters, Jerusalem, and CID Jaffa leave ten British security forces dead and twelve wounded.

1946

29 January: Irgun fighters execute an arms raid on the RAF station at Aqir near Gaza.

25 February: Combined Lehi–Irgun attacks on RAF airfields at Lydda, Kfar Sirkin and Qastina result in aircraft losses amounting to an estimated value of £2 million.

2 April: Seventy-five members of Irgun blow up five railway bridges, destroy the train station at Ashdod and sever the rail line between Haifa and Acre.

23 April: In an attack on the Ramat Gan police station, Irgun raiders seize large quantities of arms and ammunition.

10 June: The Irgun inflicts £100,000 damage on the Palestine railway network.

16–17 June: Combined Irgun–Lehi attacks destroy eleven road and rail bridges.

18 June: Irgun operatives abduct four British Army officers and one Royal Air Force (RAF) officer in Tel Aviv.

22 July: The King David Hotel in Jerusalem is bombed by the Irgun, killing ninety-one and injuring forty-six.

31 October: Irgun agents detonate two bombs in the British embassy in Rome.

17 November: A police truck detonates a landmine, killing three British policemen and an RAF sergeant.

27 December: Irgun fighter Benjamin Kimchi receives eighteen lashes as punishment handed down by a British Mandate court.

29 December: Members of the Irgun abduct four British soldiers and give each eighteen lashes.

1947

January: Irgun agents abduct retired British Army officer Major H. Collins and Judge Ralph Windham.

29 January: The British Mandate authorities introduce martial law in designated areas in Palestine.

14 February: The British government announces that it would be referring the Palestine problem to the UN General Assembly later in the year.

1 March: The Irgun conducts sixteen major attacks on British targets, killing twenty.

19 April: Irgun fighters Dov Gruner, Yechiel Dresner, Mordechai Alkahi and Eliezer Kashani are hanged by the British at Acre Prison for insurrectionist activities.

21 April: Irgun fighter Meir Feinstein and Lehi activist Moshe Barazani commit suicide while awaiting execution, blowing themselves up with a hand grenade smuggled into the prison.

26 April: A British police inspector and three constables are killed in Tel Aviv.

28 April: A special session of the UN General Assembly appoints the Special Committee on Palestine (UNSCOP).

4 May: Irgun fighters attack Acre Prison, freeing twenty-eight Irgun and Lehi members incarcerated there by the British administration.

18 July: The *Exodus 1947* docks at Haifa.

29 November: United Nations Resolution 181, 'United Nations Partition Plan for Palestine', is adopted by the body's general assembly, terminating the British mandate over Palestine.

29 July: Irgun fighters Avshalom Haviv, Meir Nakar and Yaakov Weiss are hanged by the British at Acre Prison for their role in the 4 May attack on the prison. Irgun hangs two British Army sergeants in retaliation.

30 November: The first phase of Israel's War of Independence commences.

1948

9 April: Elements of the Irgun and Lehi (Stern Gang) kill 107 Arabs in an attack on a Palestinian Arab village, Deir Yassin.

25 April: Irgun launches a massed attack on the Arab-dominated city of Jaffa.

14 May: The modern state of Israel is born.

15 May: The British mandate of Palestine ends.

June: The newly formed Israel Defence Forces (IDF) and Irgun fighters exchange fire over the fate of the *Altalena* (former landing ship, tank USS *LST-138*) used by the Irgun to ship in war matériel.

11 June: Irgun is disbanded.

INTRODUCTION

> If our dreams for Zionism should be dissolved in the smoke of the revolvers of assasins and if our efforts for its future should provoke a new wave of banditry worthy of the Nazi Germans, many persons like myself will have to reconsider the position that we have maintained so firmly for such a long time. In order to hold out a possibility for future peace, these harmful activities must cease and those responsible for them must be radically destroyed and eliminated.
>
> Winston Churchill, 17 November 1944, addressing the House of Commons days after the assasination of Lord Moyne.

In October 1944, the US Office of Strategic Services described the *Irgun Zvai Leumi* (Etzel)—National Military Organization—as

> an underground, quasi-military organization with headquarters in Palestine ... fanatical Zionists who wish to convert Palestine and Trans-Jordan into an independent Jewish state ... advocate the use of force both against the Arabs and the British to achieve this maximal political goal.

In 1925, Ze'ev Jabotinsky founded the Revisionist Zionism organization, whose non-religious, right-wing ideology would lead to the formation of the Irgun and, ultimately, of the Likud Party.

Commencing operations in the British Mandate of Palestine in 1931, the Irgun adopted a mainly protective role, while facilitating the ongoing immigration of Jews into Palestine. In 1936, Irgun guerrillas started attacking Arab targets, killing more than 250 by the end of the Second World War. The British White Paper of 1939 rejected the establishment of a Jewish nation and, as a direct consequence, Irgun fighters started targeting the British.

The authorities executed captured Irgun operatives found guilty of terrorism, while deporting hundreds to internment camps overseas. As details of Jewish genocide—the Holocaust—emerged, the Irgun declared war on the British in Palestine. Acts of infrastructural sabotage gave way to the bombing of buildings and police stations, the worst being the bombing of the King David Hotel in Jerusalem—the hub of British operations and administration—in July 1946, killing ninety-one.

They would also enact the Old Testament eye-for-an-eye law of retribution, inflicting floggings and hangings on randomly selected British military personnel in matching responses to the British punishment of Jewish underground fighters.

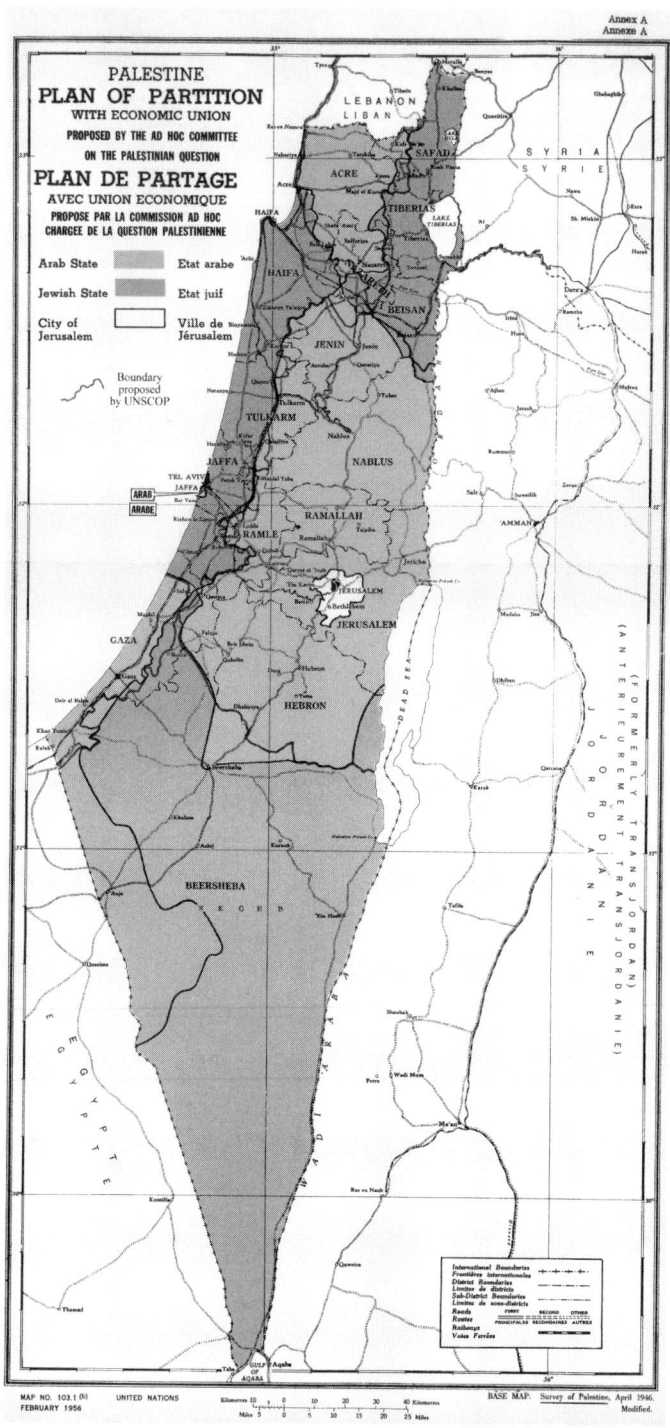

The 1947 UN plan of partition.

Introduction

Haganah, the underground military organization of the *Yishuv* (the Jewish community of Palestine) advocated restraint, a policy that the Irgun rejected entirely. Formed in 1929 as the official representative of the Jewish community within the British Mandate of Palestine, the Jewish Agency openly disassociated itself from the Irgun's militant modus operandi, frequently condemning the organization's violent activities.

Following the 1939 publication by the British government of the white paper restricting Jewish immigration in Palestine, the Irgun would forcibly challenge the British mandatory authority to ensure the establishment of a Jewish homeland: 'Eretz Israel', the Land of Israel.

During the Second World War, Irgun diverted its focus to the fight against a common scourge: Hitler's Nazi Germany. Its members enlisted in the British Army's Palestinian units, and ultimately the Jewish Brigade.

However, within months of assuming command of the Irgun in 1943, future Israeli prime minister Menachem Begin declared war on the British occupancy of Palestine. Polish by birth and a former guest of Stalin's Siberian Gulag, Begin would order many of Irgun's operations, including the bombing of the British administrative offices in Jerusalem's King David Hotel.

At this time, the Jewish Agency's and Haganah's tolerance of the Irgun's acts of terror ceased, launching instead a combined operation, codenamed *Sezon*—the Hunting Season—to neutralize the Irgun's anti-British terror campaign. But the Irgun's attacks on the British infrastructure and mandatory administration escalated, including the killing of British military personnel.

The Irgun was only dissolved after the birth of the independent Jewish state of Israel on 14 May 1948 when, in August of that year, the newly formed Israeli government issued an ultimatum: join the Israel Defence Forces (IDF) or face the violent consequences. In September 1948, Irgun was fully integrated into the IDF.

Freedom fighters or terrorists, this is their story.

1941 Poster distributed in the US by the United Palestine Appeal. (Photo Israel GPO)

1. CUSTODIANS OF ZION

> I am a Jew. I am a son of that ancient nation which thousands of years ago emerged from the obscurity of history, reaching this country, its Land of Promise, through seas and deserts and battles, establishing in it a flourishing state, making fruitful not only the fields of this country but also the idea of man and the universe. The Jewish state lays at the crossroads of international routes, a fact that explains its importance and its curse to this very day.
>
> Irgun fighter, prisoner Menachem 'Zeev' Schiff at his trial.*

For centuries, the three principle branches of the so-called Abrahamic religions—Judaism, Islam and Christianity—lay scriptural claim to the city of Jerusalem and an ill-defined Holy Land.

In the annual Jewish cycle of reading from the Torah and the seventh from the Book of Leviticus, the Land of Israel sits at the centre of the world, and Jerusalem sits at the centre of the Land of Israel (*Midrash Tanchuma Kedoshim*, Siman 10). From 1004 BC, Jerusalem has been the spiritual hub of the Jewish faith. Within the city itself is the Western Wall, remains of the Second Temple destroyed by the Romans in AD 70, constituting one of the holiest sites in Judaism. It is here on the Temple Mount that Jewish eschatology foretells the building of a Third Temple, the restoration of the House of David and the coming of the Jewish Messiah in the 'end of days'.

For the Hebrew nation, the Promised Land—Eretz Yisrael—was, according to the *Tanakh* (Hebrew Bible), given to Abraham and his descendants by God. The boundaries, however, vary according to scriptural interpretation—specifically the books of Genesis and Exodus—and tradition. Essentially, the territory stretches from the Red Sea ('Sea of Reeds'), to the Mediterranean Sea ('Sea of the Philistines'), and from the desert to the Euphrates ('the River'). The Jordan River bisects the land.

The Al-Aqsa Mosque, first constructed on Jerusalem's Temple Mount in AD 705, is the third holiest site in Islam. Translated from the Arabic as 'The Farthest Place of Prostration', according to the Qur'an, it is from here that the prophet Muhammad ascended into the heavens in a night in 620 BC. The mosque is also revered by Islam for its links to Biblical (Hebrew and Christian) prophets such as Abraham, David, Solomon, Elijah and Jesus.

---

* Eli Tavin & Yonah Alexander (eds.), *Psychological Warfare and Propaganda: Irgun Documentation* (Scholarly Resources, Washington, 1982).

For the adherents of Islam, particularly the Palestinian Arabs, the scriptures are clear as to spiritual entitlement to the Holy Land: "O my people! Enter the holy land which Allah hath assigned unto you, and turn not back ignominiously, for then will ye be overthrown, to your own ruin." (Qur'an, Surah 5 (Al-Ma'idah), Ayah 21).

In 500 BC, the Greek historians wrote of 'Palaistínē', the coastal land from Phoenicia to Egypt inhabited by 'Syrians of Palestine'. In the second century BC, the Roman conquerors adopted the word 'Palestine' for the region, using the term on coins and documents. Since the end of the Second World War, there has been a rapid expansion in Palestinian nationalist demands for an independent Palestinian state.

From Old Testament prophecies to the Messianic teachings and doctrine of Jesus in the New Testament, Jerusalem is of profound importance to the Christian faith. It was here that the Saviour Jesus was presented as a child, and where he preached and performed miracles. It was also in the city that he partook of his last supper with his disciples prior to his arrest, trial and execution on the cross. And for the world's Christians, the apocalyptic return of the Messiah will centre on Jerusalem.

From the ancient Egyptians to modern-day Israelis, Palestinians and Jordanians, the Holy Land has been controlled by Canaanites, Israelites and Judeans, Assyrians, Babylonians, Persians, Greeks, the Jewish Hasmoneans, Romans, Parthians and Sasanians, Byzantines, the Arab caliphates, Crusaders, Ayyubid sultans, Turkish Mamluk sultanates, Mongols, Ottomans, and finally the British.

The Western or Wailing Wall in Jerusalem's Old City, and upper left, the Islamic shrine, Dome of the Rock. (Photo Israel GPO)

In the early sixteenth century, the sovereign Venetian Republic in northeast Italy established a 'ghetto' in Venice, in which Jews were compelled to reside. Later that century, the Papacy determined that Jews in Rome would face similar restrictions. Seen as a much-improved method of 'managing' Jewish urban populations, especially in terms of taxation, the concept spread across much of Europe. Whilst the etymology of the word 'ghetto' remains a subject of debate, it has become assimilated into the English language, representing specific areas of residency where the inhabitants eke out a living in poverty and destitution. In the Second World War, the ghetto became an instrument for the systematic eradication of millions of Jews.

The lamentations of the people of the Kingdom of Judah, held in captivity in Babylonia after the fall of its capital, Jerusalem, is enshrined in a Psalm (*Tehillim*) of the *Tanakh*, and Psalm 137 of the Christian Bible: "By the rivers of Babylon, there we sat down, yea, we wept, when we remembered Zion ... How shall we sing the Lord's song in a strange land? ... If I forget thee, O Jerusalem, let my right hand forget her cunning. If I do not remember thee, let my tongue cleave to the roof of my mouth; if I prefer not Jerusalem above my chief joy."

With the passage of time, in Europe the diverse spectrum of political, economic and religious tolerance—or lack of—of the trans-border Jewish race, manifested itself in like measure in the birth and spread of Zionism, based on the Biblical return of the Jews from Babylonian exile to Eretz Yisrael, an act known as *Aliyah*, a foundation tenet of international Zionism.

From the zealous to the secular Jew, eastern Europe was the crucible of the first *Aliyah*, fuelled by anti-Semitic legislation and pogroms in Imperial Russia—Kiev, Odessa, Warsaw—following the assassination of Tsar Alexander II on 1 March 1881 and for which the finger of blame was pointed at the Jewish race. In the period 1882 to 1903, around 35,000 Jews migrated to a southwestern region of Syria, at the time a province of the Ottoman Empire. Those arriving in Palestine were given the sobriquet '*Hibbat Tysion*'—'enthusiasts for Zion'.

THE NEW MOSES TO LEAD THE JEWS HOME

A LIMITED LIABILITY COLONY
A new Moses has arisen, and a *Pall Mall* representative at Vienna has unearthed him. It was not in the bleak and howling wilderness, but in one of those charming mountain resorts of the jaded Viennese that our Patriarch—or Dr Theodor Herzl, as he is called for the nonce —revealed himself and his

purpose, and chatted about the biggest idea in creation. If his adherents have read destiny aright, he is the one whom the scattered and persecuted tribes of Israel have vainly sought for centuries to lead them back to the Promised Land flowing with milk and honey.

In the plainest and most prosaic of 19th century language, he has on foot the floating of a Limited Liability Company in London, with an invested capital of millions, for the purpose of acquiring Palestine and thoroughly organising it for settlement. That is the so-called Zionistic movement of to-day. Dr Herzl, according to himself, is no business man, and yet has facts and figures at his finger-ends which have won for him converts throughout the world. He proposes in one coup to settle the Anti-Semitic agitation for ever and aye, and in its stead a Jewish State, which to-day is a myth, an unknown quantity, is to startle the world by a leap into existence.

First impressions are deceptive. Dr Herzl, a tall, handsome, courteous man, is no exception. He is disappointingly phlegmatic for one with a cause that may deplete Europe in a decade or so of 10,000,000 inhabitants, and solve the most burning social question of the day. It is only when you have seen something of the hidden fires of enthusiasm that smoulder beneath the surface that you get another impression. The worthy doctor has played many parts in his time. He has practised law and written plays, and is now one of the best known journalists and literary men in Austria.

A JEWISH RHODESIA
"For founding the Jewish State," said Herzl, "my plan might be styled a Jewish Rhodesia, but with this difference, that within a year or so of Palestine being acquired from the Turk I shall have a million colonists in the country."

"How that possible?"

"We shall first send an exploring expedition, equipped with all the modern resources of science, which will thoroughly overhaul the land from one end to the other before it is colonised, and establish telephonic and telegraphic communication with the base as they advance. The old methods of colonisation will not do here. It was in Paris, three years ago, while I was the correspondent of a Vienna paper, that I first hit on the idea. I had no hopes then of ever realising it, but my return to Austria was very much like the man with the anaconda in a box, who was surprised to find that it had grown out of all proportion to its surroundings."

Dundee Evening Telegraph, Saturday, 31 July 1897

Theodor Herzl.

Following in the footsteps of earlier Zionist activists, theorists, scholars and rabbis, Austro-Hungarian journalist, author and political activist, Theodor Herzl, is today officially recognized as the spiritual father of the state of Israel. Born to secular Jews in 1860 in the Jewish quarter of Pest, Herzl read law at the University of Vienna before pursuing journalism and literature.

In February 1896, Herzl's seminal work *Der Judenstaat* (The Jews' State) was published, in which he argued that the only solution to avoid widespread anti-Semitism in Europe would be to move to Palestine, the historical Jewish homeland. Popularizing the term Zionism, a word first coined in 1890 by Austrian Jewish nationalist and journalist Nathan Birnbaum, Herzl injected life into Zionism in 1897 with the formation of the World Zionist Organization (WZO).

However, Herzl would not live to see his dream of a Zionist state in Palestine become a reality. On 3 July 1904, he died in Lower Austria of cardiac sclerosis at the age of 44. In the Declaration of the Establishment of the State of Israel proclaimed on 14 May 1948 (5 Iyar 5708) by David Ben-Gurion, executive head of the World Zionist Organization and first prime minister, paragraph four of the preamble immortalizes Theodor Herzl: "In the year 5657 (1897), at the summons of the spiritual father of the Jewish State, Theodore Herzl, the first Zionist Congress convened and proclaimed the right of the Jewish people to national rebirth in its own country."

The second *Aliyah* saw some 40,000 Jews, mainly from Russia, arrive in southwestern Syria between 1904 and the outbreak of the First World War in 1914. But by this time, the Zionist organization, now under the leadership of Herzl's successor, David Wolffsohn, was stalling. Rifts had appeared, based on increasingly divergent interpretations of Zionism. For the Orthodox Jew, his inalienable right to the Land of Israel was granted by God to the ancient Israelites of the Bible. By contrast, the largely secular socialist Zionists held that Israel would only be restored by the coming Messiah.

Meanwhile, in Ottoman Palestine Hebrew was adopted as the new lingua franca to solve the issue of the diversity of languages in everyday use by migrants arriving from the global diaspora. In 1909, construction commenced of a new city in Palestine: Tel Aviv, a name adopted from the title of the 1902 Hebrew translation of Herzl's Utopian novel, *Altneuland*—The Old New Land.

At the time of the outbreak of the First World War, continental Europe's complexion was dominated by autocratic dynastic empires: Russian, Habsburg,

German and Ottoman. Allegiances and alliances were bought and sold, ironically, to maintain an imbalance of power, resulting by 1914 in the emergence of two multinational power blocks: the German, Austro-Hungarian and Italian triple alliance, and the Franco–Russian Entente. With aspirations of re-acquiring interests in the Balkans and North Africa, the Ottoman Turks found themselves effectively in opposition to the Russians and the British. As a consequence, two months after the outbreak of war, the Turks allied themselves with the triple alliance of the Central Powers.

Britain had already by this time established a controlling interest in the rich oilfields at the head of the Persian Gulf. Just prior to the start of the war, the Turks had granted the Germans permission to construct the Baghdad Railway from the Mediterranean Sea to the Persian Gulf, bringing them in direct confrontation with the British.

Emboldened by the backing of the Central Powers that the new alliance provided, the Turks raised two armies of invasion to simultaneously march on the Balkans and Egypt. The Egyptian operation would be undertaken by 60,000 *nizam* (regular) troops and 10,000 *redif* (reservists) drawn from Syria and Palestine. The force would, in stages, be deployed along the Hedjaz railway through Jerusalem, before proceeding on foot toward the Sinai Peninsula. At the Suez Canal, however, a 50,000-strong composite force of British, Indian, Anzac and Egyptian troops—with a further 40,000 in reserve—inflicted a crushing defeat on the Turks, preventing them from crossing the canal. Elsewhere, in the Persian Gulf and Mesopotamia (now Iraq), British and Indian forces continued to push back the Turks.

By mid-1916, while bolstering east-bank defences along the Suez Canal, British forces, now under General Sir Archibald Murray, had advanced halfway across the Sinai. It was at this point that any remaining designs the Turks had of

1917 First World War Jewish recruitment poster.

invading Egypt evaporated when the Great Arab Revolt against Ottoman Turkish rule in the Hejaz commenced in June 1916. The British fully endorsed the Arab uprising initiated by the Sharif of Mecca, providing financial support, personnel (including T. E. Lawrence) and promising to recognize Arab independence after the end of the war. However, following the publication of the Balfour Declaration in November 1917, which promised the Jews a homeland in Palestine, the Arab world accused the British of reneging on the agreement contained in the eponymous McMahon–Hussein Correspondence.

On 27 June 1917, Lieutenant-General Edmund 'The Bull' Allenby succeeded Murray as commander of the Egyptian Expeditionary Force. Having been relieved of his command of the British Army on the Western Front in a show of no confidence, Allenby

THE JEWS IN JERUSALEM "NEXT YEAR"?

How This Week brings Then New Hope
By Ibn Ezra.

For close on 2,000 years Jews of all ages and in every country have concluded the Passover service by a phrase that they are using this week. That phrase may be literally translated from the Hebrew as 'Next year in Jerusalem'. In the past it has not stood for very much more than a hope unlikely to be fulfilled, excepting some catastrophic happening difficult to foresee. But this year the Passover, to every Jew who believes, is full of mystic significance and high promise.

It has been estimated that there are nearly 1,000,000 Jews fighting in the various armies distributed throughout Europe. Their record has been a good one. Their share of honours in all countries has been very high, and they have shown that the fighting spirit of the Maccabees is by no means extinct.

For some years past an earnest body of men and women have been trying to organise in some practical way the ideals that go to the making of a Zionist. It has not always been easy task, for the Jew is apt to be ultra conservative and mistrustful of hope. Never, however, has the Zionist movement been as strong as it is today. The war has brought home to the minds of millions of Jews the fact that while many little nationalities are going to liberated by this war the case of the Jews may be overlooked.

What is the ease of the Jew? It may divided into two parts: that the grievances of Jews in various countries shall not be overlooked in the final peace-making, and (b) that some definite effort shall made to secure settlement of Jews in Palestine.

Daily Mirror, Wednesday, 19 April 1916

Ottoman troops in Palestine, First World War. (Photo Israel GPO)

arrived from London without precise orders for his task ahead. Eventually, he was ordered to attack the Turks in southern Palestine. By mid-August, the strength of his force was close to 100,000, made up of the Desert Mounted, XX and XXI corps. On 24 October, Allenby launched a two-pronged attack: XXI Corps on Gaza and the Desert Mounted and XX Corps on Beersheba to the southeast.

Beersheba fell relatively quickly, but Turkish forces entrenched before Gaza tenaciously held their line, despite a brutal artillery and naval bombardment of their defensive positions. Finally, during the night of 6/7 November, Allenby's forces entered Gaza, evacuated by the Turks under cover of darkness.

A week later, Allenby took the key strategic Junction Station, the point where the railway from Beersheba links up with the Jaffa–Jerusalem line, thereby splitting the Ottoman Yildirim Army Group in two: the Eighth Army on the coast and the Seventh Army in the hills around Jerusalem. On 16 November, the New Zealand Mounted Rifles Brigade took the port city of Jaffa, allowing Allenby to fully focus on taking the Holy City.

By the end of the first week of December, Allenby was ready to attack Jerusalem itself, his fighting route having passed through ancient sites revered by Muslim, Jew and Christian alike: the Judean Hills; Beth Horon where Joshua battled the five Amorite kings; Kirjath Jearim (Kuryet al Enab), resting place of the Ark of the Covenant for twenty years before being moved into Jerusalem; and the mosque at Nebi Samwil, which houses the tomb of the prophet Samuel. Moving up from Beersheba, elements of Allenby's XX Corps entered Hebron without opposition. Known as the 'City of Abraham, the Friend of God', Hebron was King David's capital and military base as he prepared to capture Jerusalem. Moving up from the south, British troops took Bethlehem before cutting the Jericho road and securing the Mount of Olives.

As night fell on 8 December, the Ottoman army evacuated Jerusalem, followed by the city's capitulation the next day. Mayor Hussein Bey al-Husayni, a member of a prominent Jerusalem Arab family, conveyed the instruments of surrender from Izzat, Ottoman Mutasarrif of Jerusalem District, which encompassed Bethlehem, Hebron, Jaffa, Gaza and Beersheba. The text read:

> Due to the severity of the siege of the city and the suffering that this peaceful country has endured from your heavy guns; and for fear that these deadly bombs will hit the holy places, we are forced to hand over to you the city through Hussein al-Husseini, the mayor of Jerusalem, hoping that you will protect Jerusalem the way we have protected it for more than five hundred years.*

The British monarch, King George V, immediately wired his pleasure at receiving news of the capture of Jerusalem: "By skilful dispositions you have preserved intact the Holy Places."† Ancient Zion had indeed come under new custodianship.

While General Allenby continued to prosecute what had now become a costly campaign to liberate Jerusalem from Ottoman forces, in the tranquil societal and political circles of London, Hebrew Zionist Chaim Azriel Weizmann persisted in seeking the support of the British establishment for the Zionist cause.

The Russian-born biochemist and future first president of the state of Israel, Weizmann had settled in Britain in 1904 where he gained citizenship. During the British election campaign of 1905–06, Weizmann became acquainted with Conservative MP and erstwhile British prime minister, Arthur James Balfour. Appointed foreign secretary in David Lloyd George's new administration late in 1916, and in spite of Weizmann's reputation in Britain as a "radical, a man of the people", Balfour quickly warmed to the Zionist's call for a Jewish homeland in Palestine. Weizmann's charm and unlikely ability to access the corridors of power in Whitehall, resulted in Balfour even declaring that he, personally, was a Zionist.

In May 1916, in an agreement endorsed by the Russians, Britain and France entered into a secret agreement on the post-war dissection of a defeated Ottoman Empire. The architects of the plan, British Conservative politician and Middle East adviser to the war cabinet, Sir Mark Sykes, and French diplomat François Georges-Picot agreed that Syria and Lebanon would become French territories, while Palestine would be divided into French and Anglo-French zones of control. When the contents of the misguided agreement—officially known as the Asia Minor Agreement—was aired in public, the Arab world was shocked and Weizmann livid.

---

* www.firstworldwar.com
† Sir J. A. Hammerton (ed.), *A Popular History of the Great War*, Vol. IV (Fleetway House, London).

General Allenby's victorious troops on parade in Jerusalem, 1917. (Photo American Colony (Jerusalem) Photo Dept.)

In the aftermath of the ensuing months into 1917, the Foreign Office increasingly doubted the wisdom of the Anglo-French agreement on the future of Palestine. Despite anti-Zionist sentiment in certain political quarters, and concerns about Arab expectations in Palestine, on 31 October 1917 Lloyd George and his cabinet agreed to a carefully worded declaration that they believed addressed the interests of both Jew and Arab in the historically contested Palestine.

Overshadowed by the victory of Vladimir Lenin's Bolshevik October Revolution in Russia, on 9 November the outcome of the cabinet's deliberations was conveyed into the public domain by means of a letter from Balfour to French-born British Liberal politician and philanthropist Lord James de Rothschild:

Foreign Office,
November 2nd, 1917.

Dear Lord Rothschild,

I have much pleasure in conveying to you, on behalf of His Majesty's, Government, the following declaration of sympathy with Jewish Zionist aspirations, which has been submitted to and approved by the Cabinet:

His Majesty's Government view with favour the establishment in Palestine of a national home for the Jewish people, and will use their best endeavours to facilitate the achievement of this object, it being clearly understood that nothing shall be done which may prejudice the civil and religious rights of existing non-Jewish [Arab] communities in Palestine, or the rights and political status enjoyed by Jews in any other country.

I should grateful if you would bring this declaration to the knowledge of the Zionist Federation.

Yours sincerely,
Arthur James Balfour.

With the cessation of hostilities, the joint British and French military Occupied Enemy Territory Administration (OETA) was established over the Levantine and Mesopotamian provinces of the former Ottoman Empire following the Sinai and Palestine Campaign of the First World War.

In July 1920, British Liberal politician Sir Herbert Samuel was appointed as the first British High Commissioner to Palestine as head of the civilian administration to replace that of the military. A practising Jew and adherent of Zionism, Samuel would be the first Jew to govern the ancient land of Israel in 2,000 years. However,

Herbert Samuel striding into Jaffa, 1 June 1920. (Photo American Colony (Jerusalem) Photo Dept.)

head of the military government, General Allenby, and Secretary of State for Foreign Affairs (1919–24) Lord George Curzon regarded the appointment of a Zionist Jew to govern Palestine as both dangerous and premature. Arab displeasure was immediate as evidenced by a threat to blow up the train taking him to Jerusalem on the day of his arrival.

At a twelfth private meeting of the members of the Council of the League of Nations, held at St James's Palace, London, on 22 July 1922, a draft of the 'Class A Mandate of Palestine' was approved. Incorporated were the Balfour Declaration's 'national home for the Jewish people' and the creation of an Arab home, Trans-Jordan. The British mandate officially came into force on 29 September.

By this time, Palestinian Arabs had already formally rejected the Balfour Declaration and its promise of a Jewish homeland in Palestine. Meeting in Jerusalem from 27 January to 9 February 1919, Muslim and Christian delegates to the First Palestinian Arab Congress refused to accept British rule over Palestine. Arab expressions of dissension were transformed into violent riots early in 1920, aimed exclusively against Jews. In Upper Galilee, Arab mobs fell on Jewish communal settlements, including the kibbutz of Tel Hai, where Joseph Trumpeldor suffered fatal injuries while heading the defence of the village. His martyrdom became a symbol of the pre-state Zionist movement's right to self-defence and struggle for independence.

Perceiving that the British had no desire to address such attacks, the leadership of the pre-state Jewish residents of Israel—the Yishuv—looked to themselves for the defence of "Jewish life, property and honour". It was, therefore, in the wake of the 1920 Arab riots that the Haganah (lit. the defence) was established, a loosely structured citizen-soldier militia largely comprising veterans of the Jewish Legion. However, weaponry was woefully inadequate and training poor.

The Churchill White Paper of 3 June 1922, regarded by many as the earliest example of a document that sets out to provide alternative solutions to complex government issues and policies, addressed the tensions between Jews and Arabs in Palestine. Officially referred to as 'Correspondence with the Palestine Arab Delegation and the Zionist Organisation', the White Paper stressed the need for equal rights in Palestine, where neither side feels threatened or subjugated. Calling for limitations on Jewish immigration to facilitate a defusing of tensions, the White Paper heralded a tangible shift in British policy in the mandate, specifically one which banned the Haganah as an illegal organization. Determined to continue on the path of self-defence against Arab aggression, the Haganah simply went underground.

From 1922 to 1928, while tensions continued to simmer below the surface, there were no major incidents of Arab violence.

During the first few years of the twentieth century, a remarkably talented and intelligent Ukrainian-born Jew stepped onto the international Zionist stage. Journalist,

Ze'ev Jabotinsky in the uniform of the Jewish Legion, 1919. (Photo Jabotinsky Institute)

author, poet, soldier, multi-linguist, activist, orator, natural leader, he was born Vladimir Yevgenyevich Jabotinsky.

Having established the militant Jewish Self-Defence Organization to protect Jewish communities in the Russian Empire, Jabotinsky went on, together with Theodor Herzl, to form the Zion Mule Corps in the British Army during the First World War. He then served as a non-commissioned officer in the 20th Battalion, London Regiment, before the British government agreed to the formation of a Jewish combatant unit, the Jewish Legion. Raised specifically to fight the Ottoman Empire, the legion comprised five Jewish volunteer battalions: the 38th to the 42nd (Service) battalions, the Royal Fusiliers. Jabotinsky enlisted with the 38th Battalion, where he received a commission as an honorary lieutenant.

Throughout his First World War service in a British uniform, Jabotinsky fostered high expectations of the Jewish Legion assuming a role as an embryonic Jewish defence force in Palestine—reward for the Jewish volunteers contribution to the Allied war effort. As a state of peace returned to Europe and the Middle East after the defeat of the German and Ottoman empires, a frustrated Jabotinsky felt compelled to register with Allenby his displeasure about the British Army's development of an ambivalent attitude toward the Jewish Legion. To his profound dismay, shortly thereafter the Jewish Legion was disbanded and Jabotinsky appointed a Member of the Order of the British Empire, MBE. The decoration was scant consolation as Jabotinsky had lost a bespoke Jewish homeland defence force.

In 1920, Jabotinsky would spend ten weeks in the Acre Prison for his role in countering Arab riots in Jerusalem. In this period of brief incarceration, Jabotinsky reflected on his weakening faith in the British mandatory administration. The final straw came the following May when attacks on Jews in Jaffa and various kibbutzim left forty-seven Jews dead and 146 wounded. In an inquiry into the unrest, the British chief justice of Palestine, Sir Thomas Haycraft, apportioned blame on inflammatory Zionist statements and the belligerent attitude of Jewish youth in the settlements.

That September, Emir Abdullah was granted a large tract of land eastward from the Jordan River—Trans-Jordan—reducing the Palestine Mandate to 10,000 square miles. This development, without consultation from London, was approved by the Jewish Agency. The Zionists—Jabotinsky in particular—were angered by what they saw as British duplicity and Jewish Agency appeasement. By now the powerful *Histadrut*—General Organization of Workers in Israel—had virtually emasculated the now illegal Haganah, and Jewish immigration into Palestine had dropped dramatically.

For Jabotinsky, timing was now of the essence. The ancient territorial integrity of Eretz Yisrael could not and would not be allowed to be compromised by what he referred to as the "practical" Zionism of the Jewish Agency. In 1921, Jabotinsky formed the Union of Revisionist Zionists, with the prime objective of ensuring by whatever means that the Jewish homeland, including both sides of the River Jordan, would remain intact.

A member of the Betar youth movement in Europe, 1924. (Photo Jabotinsky Institute)

Over the next few years, Jabotinsky toured the Jewish diaspora in eastern Europe, actively striving for the materialization of his dream, the defining mantra of Revisionist Zionism. In 1923, Jabotinsky formed the right-wing Betar youth movement in Riga, Latvia, and by September 1924, fifty new Betar groups had been formed. From a small office in Berlin, the Betar were given uniforms and trained in weapons handling and live firing at military-style camps. Parades were staged, complete with banners, flags and special salutes, the whole stirred by patriotic poetry.

For Jabotinsky, *legyon* (legion), military training and *giyus* (lit. enlistment or induction) and national service in the new homeland, were integral to the achievement of a single Jewish state. And for the Betarim, the road to Zion demanded blood sacrifice readily given. Jabotinsky, at this juncture, however, still recognized London as the key to Zion.

In Paris in the spring of 1925, Jabotinsky and Russian Zionists who had supported him in raising the Jewish Legion in the First World War, formed the *HaTzionim HaRevizionistim*, or *HaTzohar* (lit. The Revisionist Zionists), the political wing of the Revisionist Zionist movement.

Despite the relative calm over the next three years, the 1929 events in Palestine would harden the Revisionist Zionists' resolve to resort to unilateral 'self-defence' in Palestine. In late August, Arab riots resulted in the deaths of 133 Jews and 110 Arabs

> **THE ROLE OF BRITAIN IN PALESTINE**
>
> IMPARTIAL ADMINISTRATION
> (From Our London Correspondent.) Fleet Street, Monday.
>
> Brigadier-General Sir Wyndham Deedes, who was formerly Chief Secretary to the Administration of Palestine, cleared up some misconceptions to-night regarding the position of Great Britain as the mandatory of Palestine in an address before the Victoria Institute.
>
> He confined his remarks mainly to the religious aspect, and emphasised the real role of Great Britain as the impartial administrator of a country where the interests of Moslems, Jews, and Christians are mostly divergent. Our administration there, he said, was a trusteeship on behalf of the Allies and the United States. It was never the intention to found in Palestine for the Jews a kingdom with full Statehood, but to establish a national home for them, and it was expressly provided that nothing should be done to prejudice the rights and interests of the Moslem and Christian sections of the community.
>
> The mandatory Power had to administer the country on behalf of the people now in Palestine and on behalf of the whole world. For the Moslem it had to promote a joint cultural and artistic revival, and for the Jews to establish a national home and enable them to realise the ambitions they had entertained for centuries. The debt which Christianity owed to Judaism would thereby be liquidated. In one year of Christian administration a supreme Moslem Council had been set up—a thing which was never done during the hundreds of years that the country had been under Moslem rule. The political situation to-day was infinitely better than any during the past three or four years.
>
> Sir Wyndham confessed that it was matter of considerable surprise to him that the occupation of Jerusalem and Palestine had aroused so little interest in this country or in the Church of England and Christendom at large.
>
> *Yorkshire Post and Leeds Intelligencer*, Tuesday, 6 January 1925

throughout Palestine, the latter mainly by British troops. In Hebron, two Sephardi Jews and fifty-five Ashkenazi Jews were murdered.

The unrest, which originated in Jerusalem's Old City, coincided with the convening in Zurich of the sixteenth Zionist Congress. In the absence of the majority of Jewish leaders, the Yishuv floundered without clear direction at a crucial time. In the aftermath of the bloodshed, cracks began to appear in the cohesiveness of the Haganah. Right-wing elements within the organization revived criticism of the Haganah's weak leadership and spineless policies. The socialists were at the opposite end of the spectrum, spurning any form of militancy amidst fears that a militarized Haganah would dominate the Yishuv. A member of the Haganah command, architect and future *aluf* (brigadier-general) in the IDF, Professor Yohanan Ratner, wrote in *My Life and I*:

> Today it often seems to us to be self-evident that the Haganah had to develop into a regular army, or at least that this was the universal aspiration ... but this is a superficial assumption. Nowhere has it been stated that the Haganah had to become an army, or even that it was intended from the outset to become such; till almost the last moment, certain highly influential elements held a different view.

A militant faction within the Haganah command structure, the so-called Odessa Group, blamed Haganah intransigence for failing to protect Jewish civilians during the riots. Such an unnecessary spilling of innocent Jewish blood on Palestinian soil would not be allowed to happen again.

In April 1931, Odessa-born Jewish activist and Haganah district commander of Jerusalem, Avraham Tehomi (born Zilberg), broke away from the Haganah, taking

British armoured cars on standby at the Russian Compound during the Arab riots, August 1929. (Photo American Colony (Jerusalem) Photo Dept.)

with him other district officers loyal to his cause. Branded militant and fascist by the Haganah hierarchy, Tehomi formed a new underground movement: Haganah Bet (Second Defence), also known as Irgun Yemini or Irgun Bet.

Sharing Tehomi's disdain for conservative Zionists in the Haganah, members of Betar, Revisionist Zionists and the Zionist national religious Mizrachi Party—zealous adherents of the Torah—joined the fledgling ranks of the Haganah Bet. Lacking financial support and possessing only a small quantity of dated firearms, the organization numbered a paltry three hundred. And thus was born the *Irgun Zvai Leumi*, (National Military Organization), under the leadership of Avraham Tehomi until 1937. Leading founder members included future commander David Raziel, Avraham Stern, who would later form a splinter group in the Irgun—*Lohamei Herut Yisrael* (Lehi)—and Lithuanian-born Hillel Kook.

The Irgun, while listing its aims as a return to Zion, national freedom and independence, social justice, and freedom and happiness of the individual, in concluding paragraphs to a statement on 'aims and methods', the organization declared:

> There is no other way to free our Homeland and redeem our nation except the way of the *Liberation War*. A national Liberation War is a *just* war, which is conducted by an oppressed people against a foreign Power that has enslaved it and its country.
>
> And whereas the foreign Power is occupying the conquered country by the sheer force of its arms—for otherwise it would have been expelled overnight—it is unavoidable that the Liberation War should become a war by arms, a war by force of weapons, the weapons of freedom against those of enslavement. The Force, which the oppressed people sets up to wage war against the oppressor, is called the *Liberation Army. The Irgun is the Liberation Army of the Hebrew Nation*.
>
> Thus victory was gained by our Maccabees; thus the Italians defeated the Austrians in the 19th century; thus the Balkan peoples overcame the Turks in that same century; thus also, in the Second World War, did the European Underground Armies hasten the victory of their peoples and secure for them the fruits of victory.
>
> Without an army every people—even a great one—becomes what our own people has been: *a victim of massacres and pogroms during two thousand years*. Parties, institutions, *political movements*—all these the Hebrew people did possess in abundance; the one thing it did *not* have, one which it needs like air to breathe—is an *Army*. This was understood by the founders of 'Irgun', and therefore they did not establish a political-revolutionary group nor a defence organisation nor a new 'movement' but an *Army*. The *first* Hebrew Army, with its commanders and soldiers, its objectives and internal regime—after two thousand years of Exile.*

---

* Tavin & Alexander.

2. THE HEBREW SOLDIER

> And while the Irgun Zvai Leumi's chiefs asked for an open fight against the British, Jewish Agency leaders greeted each new disappointment with an appeal for further collaboration. While the watchword of the Irgun became 'Attack', the slogan of the Haganah remained 'Restraint'.
>
> Irgun statement.*

The sourcing of additional firearms was a priority for the Irgun's new commanders. Tehomi personally travelled to Finland to acquire Suomi KP/-31 9mm submachine guns—later copied by the Soviets as the PPSh-41—while other weapons were smuggled into Palestine, purchased from Arabs or pilfered locally.

Over the next three years, Irgun numbers swelled to 3,000, allowing for the establishment of training schools at Tel Aviv, Jerusalem and Haifa. At the seventeenth World Zionist Congress in Basel in 1931, the Revisionists now comprised 21 percent of the delegates, numbers bolstered by a greater acceptance of militant means to liberate Palestine from the British.

Jewish defiance of the British Mandate and disobedience of its laws started to surface, albeit in isolated, peaceful and relatively minor actions. At the close of Yom Kippur in 1930, activist Rabbi Moshe Halevi Segal sounded the Shofar (ram's horn) at the Kotel, the Western or Wailing Wall in Jerusalem's Old City, a religious act strictly forbidden by the British administration.

In October that year, the Passfield White Paper was issued by British colonial secretary Lord Passfield (Sidney Webb), placing significant restrictions on Jewish immigration into the mandate. In a display of passive resistance, hundreds of Jews challenged British authority by refusing to comply with the White Paper's requirement for all Palestinian Jews to be counted in a census. They opted for incarceration instead.

For Jabotinsky, the Basel conference failed in its obligation to accelerate pressure on the British 'decolonization' of Palestine to make way for an independent state of Israel. In Warsaw on 28 December 1931, in a speech translated by the Jabotinsky Institute, Jabotinsky chillingly warned London of the real danger it would face should it persist in its policies and mandatory possession of Palestine:

> England is no longer inspired by her old lust for building and leading. And what we ask of the English is, indeed, this lust and resolution, the capacity for

---

* Ibid.

The shofar, in this case a kudu horn, sounding Yom Kippur evening prayers at the Western Wall in Jerusalem. (Photo Israel GPO)

more courageous, more creative action, which is the indispensable prerequisite for the establishment of a colonization regime with the object of carrying the mandate into reality.

If conditions remain as they are, there will come into being, in Zionism, a new form of movement which will take all things into account. The effect of this situation will, no doubt, be that it will become as uncomfortable for England to rule Palestine as it is for the Jews of Palestine to be ruled by her. All this is liable to cost our people a great deal of further suffering; but I am afraid we will have to pay for England's action in Palestine.*

With the ascendency of far-right German National Socialism and the demise of the Weimar Republic in 1933, an event on a Tel Aviv beach on the night of 16 June 1933 would cement the irreconcilable ideological differences within Zionism. Ukrainian-born Yishuv Zionist leader and head of the Jewish Agency's political department, Chaim (Victor) Arlosoroff, had been visiting Nazi Germany to discuss the safety and future of an estimated 550,000 German Jews, the so-called Ha'avara Agreement. The Labour Zionists under David Ben-Gurion held that only the young and fit should come to Palestine, whereas Jabotinsky's Revisionist Zionists maintained that Palestine was for all Jews on the diaspora. Furthermore, the Labour Zionists pursued a peaceful settlement with the British, while the Revisionists distrusted the British implicitly.

---

* Jabotinsky Institute.

The Hebrew Soldier

The British army Balaklava Camp, Jerusalem, 1936. (Photo Israel GPO)

Around the time of the First World War, Arlosoroff, at the time living in Berlin, had had a relationship with a German divorcee, Magda Friedlander. On his return to Germany in 1933 to meet with Nazi officials, Arlosoroff discovered that Magda had remarried, this time to none other than Hitler's propaganda minister, Joseph Goebbels. Arlosoroff would then dedicate his full attention to meeting Magda to persuade her to facilitate a meeting with Goebbels. Arlosoroff was able to make contact with his former lover, and the understandably cautious Frau Goebbels agreed to meet him, but only after the Zionist Congress in Warsaw in four weeks' time.

At Warsaw, the intolerance between the Revisionists and the Zionist Workers' Party escalated into outright enmity. However, Ben-Gurion was stunned when informed by Arlosoroff that he intended to jump into bed with Goebbels, whose hatred of Jews was second only to that of Hitler himself. However, Arlosoroff never did meet Magda. She passed on a message indicating that the ramifications of such a meeting would be too dangerous to contemplate—for both of them.

Two days after returning to Palestine, Arlosoroff and his wife Sima were strolling along a Tel Aviv beach when an unknown assailant shot Arlosoroff in the chest. He succumbed to the wound in hospital a short while later. Within the Jewish leadership, an accusing finger was immediately pointed at the Revisionists, but the identity of those responsible for the assassination would remain a mystery. The rift

Irgun: Revisionist Zionism 1931–1948

between the Revisionists and mainstream conventional Zionism, both in Palestine and internationally, was now irreparable, with the result that the Revisionists formed their own Zionist movement—the New Zionist Organization (NZO)—in Vienna in September 1935.

Frustrated with what he perceived as Yishuv leadership intransigence and appeasement, Jabotinsky looked to Europe, where the spectre of the swastika increasingly threatened the very existence of the Jewish race on the continent. In Germany Jews often enjoyed financial resources with which to determine their own destiny, particularly when it came to the acquisition of travel visas to escape the country. In Poland, however, the lot of its 3.5 million resident Jews was largely characterized by unemployment, poverty, slums and state-institutionalized anti-Semitism. For the ambitious Jabotinsky, here was an opportunity to populate Palestine with *millions* of unwanted Jews from Poland, for which Poland would supply the NZO with weapons, and provide military training to members of the Polish Betar and officers from Palestine. An unwritten alliance evolved, and April 1940 was set as a date for the commencement of NZO-controlled illegal immigration—Aliyah Bet—of Polish Jews into Palestine.

A group of British soldiers and a wife in Jerusalem inspect a Vickers machine gun, 1936. (Photo Israel GPO)

However, Jabotinsky would not wait. During 1936 and 1937, the NZO worked on establishing the migration channel. In Palestine, Jabotinsky's son and commander of the Palestinian Betar, Ari, would control the clandestine receiving mechanism and absorption of illegal migrants into the Yishuv. In Europe, delegated members of the NZO purchased seagoing vessels, established safe and reliable contacts, and sourced necessary documentation. After 1938, the Revisionists had secreted an estimated 40,000 Aliyah Bet into Palestine.

Toward the end of 1935, five Palestinian Arab parties submitted a joint petition to the British mandatory administration, calling for an end to the sale of land to Jewish settlers and a cessation of Jewish immigration. Not only was there significant concern in the Arab community of Jewish hegemony in Palestine, but they were also aware that Revisionists were smuggling arms into Palestine.

In April 1936, six factional Palestinian Arab leaders set aside their differences to form the Arab Higher Committee (AHC) to safeguard Arab interests in the mandate. The movement was led by the British-appointed mufti of Jerusalem, Haj Amin al-Husseini, revered by Palestinian Muslims for his anti-Jewish and anti-British stance. The influential body immediately called for a general strike of Arab labour and a boycott of Jewish goods.

British soldiers on Jerusalem's Mamilla Street, 1936. (Photo Israel GPO)

Over the ensuing months until November, in what became known as the first stage of the 'Arab Revolt', Jaffa became a hot bed of Arab agitation. On 29 April, nine Jews were killed by Arab rioters, before a large mob marched on Tel Aviv, where Royal Air Force armoured cars from Ramele fired on the crowd to restore a semblance of order.

Elsewhere in the mandate, random Arab attacks on Jewish soft targets continued, resulting in the deaths of eighty-nine Jews in the first six months of the unrest. For the Revisionists, the British were complicit in the ongoing anti-Jewish violence. However, in June the British raised a 22,000-strong auxiliary police force—Notrim—for the protection of Jewish settlements, a development welcomed by the Haganah.

Early in October, the intervention of regional Arab allies Emir Abdullah of Trans-Jordan, King Ghazi of Iraq, and King Abdul Aziz ibn Saud of Saudi Arabia exerted pressure on the AHC to call off the strike. Official communiqués revealed that the unrest had left 195 Arabs dead and 804 wounded, eighty-nine Jews killed and 300 wounded, sixteen police killed and 102 wounded, and twenty-one military personnel killed and 104 wounded.

By this time, the British Army had assumed responsibility from the RAF for security in the mandate. Lieutenant-General John Dill was appointed General Officer Commanding (GOC) of the British forces in Palestine on 8 September 1936. The 2nd and 16th British infantry brigades were dispatched to Palestine on garrison duty, with the 14th Infantry Brigade replacing the 2nd in April 1938. The two remaining brigades would still be in Palestine at the outbreak of the Second World War. The 14th Infantry Brigade comprised the 1st Battalion, The Royal Scots (The Royal Regiment), the 1st Battalion, The Border Regiment, and the 2nd Battalion, The Black Watch (Royal Highland Regiment). The 16th Infantry Brigade was made up of the 2nd Battalion, The Queen's Own Royal West Kent Regiment, the 1st Battalion, The Manchester Regiment, and the 2nd Battalion, The Royal Ulster Rifles.

During these riots, the Irgun and the Haganah stood together in the defence of Jewish settlements from Arab attack.

Still holding out for British permission to raise a Jewish battalion to defend the Yishuv, in the early stages of the riots Jabotinsky shared the Jewish Agency's passive defence policy of restraint, or *havlaga*. However, in May 1937 the Irgun leader, Avraham Tehomi, believing that the original reasons for the formation of the Irgun no longer pertained, returned to the Haganah, taking with him most of the weapons and senior personnel. Whilst this was a staggering blow to the Irgun, activist groups and the young members of the Betar remained loyal to the organization.

In mid-November 1936, the Peel Commission—officially A Royal Commission on Palestine—arrived in Palestine, tasked by Whitehall to identify the causes of the Arab Revolt and to recommend lasting solutions. Led by Lord Robert Peel, the

> **SPECTACULAR BOMBING IN PALESTINE**
>
> Troops' Field Day
> Arab Rebels Refuse to be Dislodged
> Hidden In Lairs
> JERUSALEM, Thursday.
>
> Spectacular bombing and machine-gun operations were carried on by the Loyal (North Lancashire) Regiment, assisted by three aeroplanes, on the slopes of Mount Carmel to-day in an effort to dislodge rebels from their lairs.
>
> The British forces on returning to Haifa to-night, however, reported that they had not succeeded in actually locating the bands they were searching for, and could not state whether there had been any casualties. It was reported that a band of 200 rebels or more had collected on Mt. Carmel, and the troops were immediately despatched to that area. Trench mortars as well as rifles and machine-guns were used, while aeroplanes, flying low, dropped bombs and swooped down over the wooded gullies in which the rebels were believed to be lurking.
>
> A lorry with the invitation "Come on Ahmed" also patrolled the area armed with a machine-gun, but the Arabs were not to be caught napping, and declined the invitation.
>
> **APPEAL TO END STRIKE**
> The Arab Higher Committee to-day received the final text of the proposed appeal of the four Arab rulers to bring the Arab strike and campaign of violence to an end. The Committee thereupon held a meeting, and decided to confer with the district committees separately to-morrow and on Saturday in order to seek their opinions before publishing the appeal. The Sheikh Kamel Hassan, King Ibn Baud's Envoy, who returned here yesterday from Cairo, where he had been in communication with the King through the Hedjaz Legation there, resumed consultations with the Arab Higher Committee this morning, and a much more optimistic feeling prevails in Jerusalem to-day. It is even suggested that the strike may terminate during the week-end.—Press Association.
>
> *Belfast News-Letter*, Friday, 9 October 1936

commission's report, published on 7 July 1937, recommended the termination of the British mandate and the partitioning of Palestine into an Arab and a Jewish state. This was anathema to nationalist Arab and Revisionist Jew alike.

Above: British soldiers on a military vehicle fitted with a Lewis machine gun, pass the citadel in Jerusalem during the Arab unrest in 1936. (Photo Israel GPO)

Left: Lord Robert Peel leaving the King David Hotel in Jerusalem, 1936. (Photo Matson Photo Service)

This would foment further Arab violence. In September 1936, in a *World Jewry* editorial, the Irgun voiced the fact that it had had enough:

> We went with England. She has broken faith. She has spurned us. She has forsaken us. Men will phrase it in a hundred ways. No more pleading, no more piteous telegrams, no more marching up Scopus to the High Commissioner. No more cap in hand to Whitehall. The roads separate. We must go forward without England, against England. The Royal [Peel] Commission does not exist for us. Palestine is not a British territory, and we must unmake British claims to rule our land. We stand at another Masada.
> "Here we stand, we have no other way."

With Tehomi and his adherents out of the way, Jabotinsky assumed leadership of the Irgun as its commander-in-chief. While on a visit to South Africa, on 30 April 1937 he sent a telegram to his staff in Palestine: "This is my order under the prevailing conditions: if the riots are renewed and there is a tendency to attack Jews as well, do not hold back." The word *havlaga* would no longer appear in the Irgun's lexicon.

Jabotinsky appointed Colonel Robert Bitker as the Irgun's first commanding officer soon after Tehomi's departure. Newly arrived in Palestine, Warsaw-born Bitker was conscripted into the Polish Army at the age of nineteen, before fleeing to Russia where he served in the Russian White Army during the 1917 Revolution. He subsequently moved to Shanghai, where he joined the Revisionist Zionist movement and was one of the originators of the Jewish Battalion in the volunteer corps in Shanghai, which was commanded by the British. He also assumed command of Betar in southern China.

Bitker set up a new command, with Moshe Rosenberg as his chief-of-staff. As regional commanders, he appointed David Raziel in Jerusalem, with Avraham Stern as his second-in-command, secretary of the high command Charnoch Kalay in Haifa, and Aaron Haichman in Tel Aviv, the Irgun's stronghold. Betar units were also raised in outlying NZO settlements. The Irgun 'force' now numbered eighteen hundred.

By August 1937, it had become clear that Bitker was not fit for purpose. Notwithstanding the fact that he was not conversant in Hebrew, personal financial issues, personality clashes with numerous staff members, and the mysterious circumstances behind the apparent murder of Irgun member Zvi Frankel, resulted in Bitker's permanent departure to the United States. He was succeeded by Moshe Rosenberg.

The assassination by Arab gunmen in Nazareth on 26 September 1937 of the British district commissioner for Galilee, Lewis Andrews, ignited a fresh round of anti-Jewish and anti-British Arab violence in Palestine. The British authorities immediately banned the AHC and issued a warrant for the arrest of the chief suspect, Jerusalem mufti Haj Amin al-Husseini. Other members of the committee

Irgun: Revisionist Zionism 1931–1948

Above: David Raziel, left, and Avraham Stern. (Photos Israel GPO)

were jailed. The consequence of the British clampdown was that far more radical *fedayeen* began infiltrating the leadership structures of the Arab nationalist movements.

Although Jabotinsky had authorized retaliatory operations in August 1937, in spite of Arab bombing, sniping and attacks on Jewish settlements, the Irgun tended not to hit back, leaving the British security forces to fight the *fedayeen*. In early September there was an incident of reprisal when, following the murder of three Jews, the Irgun launched a counterattack, killing thirteen Arabs.

But 14 November 1937 would be embedded in the Irgun's annals as the day on which the *havlaga* ended. Dubbed 'Black Sunday', it was on this day that Jerusalem's Irgun commander, David Raziel, in a planned operation endorsed by Jabotinsky, launched retaliation attacks on selected Arab targets throughout Palestine. Raziel explained his rationale for a change in Irgun tactics:

> Defensive actions alone can never succeed. If the objective of the war is to break the will of the enemy—and this cannot be achieved without shattering their power—we clearly cannot be content with defensive action. Purely defensive tactics will never break the enemy's strength.

MORE KICKS THAN HA'PENCE

Dr. Weizmann, President of the Zionist Organization, declared at the Zionist Congress at Zurich yesterday that not only had Britain lacked firmness in her administration of the Palestine Mandate, but that the British Army in Palestine had been little more than a spectator during the Arab troubles.

To those who have interpreted the mandate correctly—as we believe—as a system designed to maintain an impartial balance between the two races in Palestine, Dr. Weizmann's first statement will seem unfair, and the second one nothing less than impudent. The failure of the Palestine Mandate has nothing whatever to do with any effete element in British trusteeship. It has been brought about by a complete change in the conditions in a territory upon which the mandate was originally imposed; conditions which have outgrown and made unsuitable a mandate which was never intended to be permanently rigid in its application.

European events in recent years—in Poland, Germany, and Rumania particularly—have imposed upon the mandate system, because of the enormous impetus given to Jewish immigration, a sudden strain never anticipated when originally the mandate plan was conceived. Nor is it good enough to protest, as Weizmann did, that "Jews and Arabs have worked together through the ages," with the inference that such harmony might again be possible under the existing Mandate. There was indeed such collaboration; but never was it entered into by Arabs roused by the new conviction—a wrong one, but nevertheless sufficient to light the torch of nationalism—that they might ultimately be elbowed out of their land. And just as their outlook has changed with time so has it become necessary to discard a form of administration no longer adequate in favour of partition.

We reject absolutely Dr. Weizmann's charge that the British Army did little or nothing. Zionists will know that this time last year, when the embers of Arab oppositionism were fanned to fanaticism, there was a saying among Arab nationalists that "If British influence is withdrawn from Palestine to-night, not one Jew will see to-morrow's sundown." This is heady enough talk, but at least it illumines the vendetta spirit that has been kept reasonably within bounds—despite spasmodic terrorism solely by army vigilance. This vigilance cost Britain considerable money and some lives. We will put it no higher than that. But if British impartiality is not to be tested unnecessarily it will be just as well if there is a future modification of speeches such as that delivered at Zurich yesterday

Portsmouth Evening News, Thursday, 5 August 1937

Irgun: Revisionist Zionism 1931–1948

Armed British police march along Tel Aviv's sea front during the unrest in 1937. (Photo Israel GPO)

Such a method of defence, which enables the enemy to attack as he sees fit and to retreat at will, to reorganize and to attack again—such defence is known as 'passive defence' and ends in defeat and ruin.

All these calculations lead to one conclusion: he who does not wish to be defeated must attack. The same applies to the combatants, who have no intention of oppressing others but are fighting for their own freedom and honour. They too have but one possible path – attack. They must attack their enemy and break its strength and its will.*

Operating in three-man hit squads—one to carry the weapon to the scene, one to use the weapon and the third to remove the weapon from the scene afterwards—ten Arabs were killed.

The Jewish Agency came out in immediate condemnation of the Irgun's actions, accusing the Revisionists of derailing the whole peace negotiation process. Disquiet

---

* www.etzel.org.il

descended on the diaspora and the Revisionist groups, forcing the Irgun to revert to restraint in the face of Arab provocation. Barely five months later, however, a few Jewish militants would not only shatter the tenuous *havlaga*, but their unilateral actions would plunge the British headlong onto the Irgun's battlefield for a homeland as a new enemy.

On 28 March 1938, a gang of Arabs ambushed a taxi on the Haifa–Safed road. The driver and all four Jewish passengers, including two women, were killed. In the absence of security, the perpetrators evaporated back into the surrounding hills and villages. Two weeks later, in a further car ambush, this time on the Hanita–Nahariya road, three Jews were shot and killed, including David Ben-Gaon, a graduate of the Betar battalion at the village of Rosh Pina in Upper Galilee.

Shlomo Ben-Yosef. (Photo Israel GPO)

At Rosh Pina, three outraged Betar members of the village labour battalion took it upon themselves to avenge the Jewish murders. On 21 April 1938, Ukrainian-born Shlomo Ben-Yosef (born Shalom Tabachnik), 24, Avraham Shein, 17, and Yehoshua (Shalom) Zurabin, 19, armed with a vintage revolver and an old hand grenade, ambushed an Arab bus on the road to Tiberias. However, the grenade that was lobbed to disable the bus's engine and cause it to crash over the side of the road, failed to detonate.

The three were arrested shortly afterwards and put on trial before the British military court in Haifa. Shein and Ben-Yosef were found guilty of discharging a firearm and carrying firearms, bombs and ammunition, while the charges against Zurabin were dropped on the grounds of insanity. The British administration viewed the bungled attack on the Arab bus as an act of terrorism. Justice had to be seen to be done and Shein and Ben-Yosef were both sentenced to death. Upon receipt of his birth certificate from Poland to prove that he was not yet 18 years old, Shein's death sentence was commuted to life imprisonment. He would be released in 1946.

However, for Ben-Yosef there would be no such reprieve. Appeals for clemency poured in from across the Jewish diaspora and from the Polish government, but to no avail. The British were determined, especially in the midst of major civil unrest,

British soldiers in the plaza outside Damascus Gate, Old City of Jerusalem, during Arab rioting against Jews, 1938. (Photo Israel GPO)

to make an example of Ben-Yosef, while providing the ultimate deterrent against acts of terrorism. Even Chief Rabbi Herzog's appeal to have the execution date of 29 June pushed back by one day was rejected. The day was Rosh Hodesh, a minor holiday to celebrate the first day of every month of the Hebrew calendar, and therefore no rabbi would be able to give the condemned consolation.

On the eve of his execution at Acre Prison, Ben-Yosef told journalists that he did not need consoling and that he was proud to be the first Jew to go to the gallows: "In dying I shall do my people a greater service than in life. Let the world see that Jews are not afraid to face death."

The fallout from Ben-Yosef's execution flooded Palestine and the diaspora. In Tel Aviv and Jerusalem shops closed with black cloth draped on windows as the Yishuv mourned. Following demonstrations in Tel Aviv, the British administration imposed curfews in Tel Aviv and Jerusalem. In Poland, synagogues were packed with fasting mourners, while in Lithuania, all Jewish theatres closed.

The Irgun now had a martyr to endorse their cause. Arab activists saw the execution as proof that the British administration was on their side once more, a licence to increase their attacks on the Yishuv. The British had set an example, but in doing so

> **ARABS TO STAGE BIG SUNDAY DISPLAY**
>
> LOYALTY TO KING: THANKS TO BRITISH ARMY
> Many thousands of loyal Arabs are to hold a monster demonstration in Palestine tomorrow to express their loyalty to the King and the British Government. The demonstration is planned to take place in the morning near Yatta, a hillside village to the south of Hebron. It will be coupled with a public expression of thanks to the British Army for ridding Palestine of lawless elements.
>
> BEDOUINS TOO
> Fakhri Bey Nashashibi, acting leader of the Arab defence party, who opposes the Mufti's faction, is the leader of the demonstration. In an interview yesterday he said: "You will see such a manifestation of loyalty to Britain as has not been seen since the British occupation. Many thousands of Arabs will take part, including Bedouins riding on camels and on horseback."
>
> Major-General R. N. O'Connor, military commander of Jerusalem, and Mr Edward Keith-Roach, District Commissioner of Jerusalem, as well as other army officers and a number of pressmen were invited yesterday to be present under the escort of armoured cars and British troops. Arab buses were seen in the streets of Jerusalem yesterday afternoon for the first time since the Arab transport strike began on November 1 as a protest against the regulation providing that all travellers outside towns and all drivers of cars must carry military permit passes. A large number of Arab taxis began plying in Jerusalem yesterday also. It is understood that a growing number of Arab owners and drivers are applying for the military car permits and travel passes in view of the relaxation of terrorist pressure.
>
> *Dundee Courier*, Saturday, 17 December 1938

had unwittingly unleashed widespread anti-British violence in the mandate. To the Revisionists, Britain had thrown down the gauntlet to become an enemy even greater than the Arab radicals.

In an ironic twist of fate, not lost on the Yishuv, Ben-Yosef's British hangman, police Inspector Evelyn Thomas Turton, sustained severe injuries in a Stern Gang (Lehi) bombing in 1942. His legs had to be amputated, but he never recovered, dying a week later on 21 January.

Irgun: Revisionist Zionism 1931–1948

In the 9 June 1938 edition of the *British Western Morning News and Daily Gazette*, it was reported that the British government's annual Palestine Mandate report for 1937 to the League of Nations stated that

> public security in Palestine was seriously disturbed by a campaign of murder intimidation, and sabotage conducted by Arab lawbreakers, which on a few occasions provoked Jewish reprisals. The terrorist campaign took the form of isolated murder and attempted murder; of sporadic cases of armed attacks on military, police, and civilian road transport; on Jewish settlements, and on both Arab and Jewish private property; while in the autumn there was a revival of lawlessness and violence by armed Arab bands which persisted until the end of the year.

The report added that the total casualties during the year as a result of 'terrorist and gang activities' were ninety-seven killed and 149 wounded. Of the civilian casualties, forty-four Arabs were killed and fifty-three wounded, and thirty-two Jews killed and eighty-three wounded.

In July 1938, Irgun commander David Raziel began his ruthless campaign of retaliation and retribution against Arab terror which, for him, the British were wholly impotent at addressing.

British soldiers bar entry to the Temple Mount in the Old City of Jerusalem during the curfew imposed after Arab rioting, 1938. (Photo Israel GPO)

David Raziel (born Rozenson), Russian by birth, in Belorussia (now Belarus), arrived in Ottoman Palestine in 1914 at the age of three when his parents immigrated. Upon leaving senior school, Raziel studied for several years at the Mercaz HaRav national Hebrew *yeshiva* (traditional religious institute) in Jerusalem. He then enrolled in the Hebrew University of Jerusalem where he read philosophy and mathematics. It was at this time, following the 1929 Hebron massacre, that he joined the Haganah. He subsequently became a founding member of the Irgun, becoming the organization's first commander of the Jerusalem district in 1937. The following year, Raziel succeeded David Rosenthal as commander-in-chief of the Irgun, in a move that many saw as an ousting of the moderate and 'over-cautious' incumbent who was away in Cyprus on business. A devout Jew, Raziel immediately provided robust spiritual and military leadership, for whom liberation could only be achieved with the sword. He saw the Palestinian Arabs as *dreck*, dirt to be treated as such. His inspiration fostered fervent loyalty from the Irgun rank and file who, without reservation, followed him underground.

On Monday, 4 July, two Arab passengers were killed and nine wounded, five seriously, when a bomb was thrown at an Arab bus travelling through the Jewish quarter of Western Jerusalem. In another bombing, three Arabs were killed in the Jaffa–Tel Aviv boundary zone, resulting in the introduction of a daytime curfew from 9 a.m.

Show of strength. British troops march through the streets of Jerusalem, 1938. (Photo American Colony (Jerusalem) Photo Dept.)

Two days later, an Irgun fighter, disguised as an Arab porter, deposited two milk cans filled with explosives in the busy Haifa open-air fresh-produce market, before melting away into the throng of traders and shoppers. An official statement listed the casualties as eighteen Arabs and five Jews killed, and sixty people injured. In the ensuing mêlée, rioting broke out, resulting in police reinforcements establishing order by the use of live fire. On 7 July, two people were seriously wounded in a bomb explosion in Jerusalem's Old City. The incident took place at the spot where two Jews had been killed two days before. Elsewhere in Jerusalem, at Jaffa Gate four Arabs were killed and nineteen wounded when a bomb was thrown at an Arab bus in this busy quarter of the city.

The British cruiser HMS *Emerald*, homeward bound from the East Indies, was diverted to Haifa to help deal with the crisis, pending the arrival of the battle cruiser HMS *Repulse* the following day. In Cairo, the 1st Battalion, Irish Guards, and 1st Battalion, Essex Regiment, prepared for deployment to Palestine.

Over the next few days Arab shops remained closed in Haifa in protest, and as violence spiralled out of control, twenty-two-hour curfews were imposed on the town of Tulkarem, north of Jaffa, and Nazareth.

A British marine on guard at the docked HMS *Repulse*, Haifa, 1938. (Photo Eric Matson)

Following a day of relative calm, on 10 July a large section of Haifa's main road, the Kingsway, was cordoned off by steel-helmeted marines from HMS *Repulse* to prevent an angry Arab mob from entering the Jewish quarter following the harmless explosion of a bomb near the Arab vegetable market. Eight occupants of a Jewish bus were injured when a bomb exploded inside the vehicle as it was leaving Haifa. Following the explosion, shots were fired at the bus from a nearby hillside. The driver of the bus returned fire with his revolver, and the assailants fled. In a separate incident, sixteen civilians were injured, some seriously, when a bomb was thrown at a Jewish bus in the residential quarter of the town.

At Haifa harbour, naval and army personnel unloaded emergency rations for the various naval pickets sited throughout the town, while the advance parties of British infantry ordered from Cairo arrived.

Meanwhile, in Jerusalem the leadership of several Jewish organizations, including the Histadrut (labour union) and the Jewish Labour Party, dedicated all their endeavours to curb the activities of the underground Jewish militants. They condemned the violence, calling for a return to restraint to enable a restoration of "general security".

On Friday, 15 July, an Irgun fighter lobbed a bomb—most likely from a rooftop—into the David Street Arab market in the Old City of Jerusalem, killing ten Arabs, including three women, and wounding a further twenty-nine. Ironically, security had been increased in the area following the recovery of an arms cache at the Mosque of Oman. British troops, with fixed bayonets were immediately posted at the city's main exits, and at Jaffa Gate a machine-gun emplacement was established. The authorities re-imposed the 6 p.m. curfew.

The fruit and vegetable market in Haifa sustained a massive explosion on 25 July, close to the site of the bomb blast of 6 July. Reportedly caused by a landmine detonated by members of the Irgun, *Central News Jerusalem* said that the explosion had killed thirty-five Arab civilians and wounded sixty. In the resultant chaos, angry Arab mobs set fire to Jewish shops and property, forcing the authorities to impose a twenty-four-hour curfew as Royal Marines from *Repulse* and the police scoured the town looking for the perpetrators. The immediate aftermath was described by the administration as "tense but under control".

The following day, the Irgun planned a similar act in the Old City. Eighteen-year-old Yaakov Raz volunteered to plant the device in an operation that had been drawn up some time back. Dressed up as an Arab, Raz strode into the market place carrying a basket of vegetables which concealed the mine. What the Irgun had failed to take into account, however, was that the Arab traders had closed their shops in protest against the Irgun's campaign of violence. His very act of placing the basket by a locked stall immediately made Arab bystanders suspicious. Upon investigation, the mine was discovered and the incensed Arabs set on the Irgun fighter with their knives.

Irgun: Revisionist Zionism 1931–1948

A British checkpoint on the boundary between Jaffa and Tel Aviv, 1938. (Photo Israel GPO)

Police details rushed the severely wounded Raz to the Hadassah hospital before transferring him to the government hospital where, for a fortnight, he was interrogated by British military intelligence and detectives. In his weakened state Raz feared that he might divulge information that could prove detrimental to the Irgun's very existence. It is said that he opened his wounds and bled to death in an act of sacrificial defiance, making him an inspirational hero of the Irgun cause.

By 1938, the Haganah, influenced by future Chindit commander, Orde Wingate, had become more militant. Serving at the time as an intelligence officer in the British Mandate, the pro-Zionist, anti-Arab Wingate received the necessary authority to raise combined British Army and Haganah Special Night Squads, tasked with ambushing Arab saboteurs and raiding their village bases.

However, commander of the commando-styled units, Eliyahu Golomb, did not subscribe to the Irgun's counter-terrorist activities. Despite an attempt in September by Golomb and Jabotinsky to establish a 'separate-but-equal' alliance, mutual distrust of the other's modus operandi persisted, to the extent that the two underground organizations remained polarized. Members of the Haganah disassociated themselves from Raziel's antagonistic terror tactics, while those of the Irgun held disdain for the Haganah's lack of militancy and therefore demanded to retain their freedom of

British soldiers in the Jewish Quarter of the Old City of Jerusalem with the Dome of the Rock in the background. (Photo Israel GPO)

operation. As a consequence, Jabotinsky became increasingly marginalized when military policies were formulated, even to the extent that he was not included in the planning of a sourcing expedition to Poland.

In 1938, year-on-year casualties in the prevailing unrest had escalated dramatically to 1,997 killed and 1,720 wounded. In figures released by the British government, 486 Arab civilians and 1,138 Arab 'bandits' had been killed, compared to 292 Jews, sixty-nine British civilians, policemen and troops, and twelve 'others'.

As 1938 drew to a close, the British military had taken control of Jerusalem and placed all road traffic within the mandate under strict security control. Cross-border infiltration tapered off, and against a backdrop of in-house disagreement and finger-pointing, Arab fervour in the perpetuation of the revolt started to noticeably wane. The British military cleared the hills of rebel strongholds as the administration tightened its martial grip on the mandate. The long and costly campaign to quell the Arab insurrection was starting to show signs of success.

For the Irgun, now identifying themselves as an underground army, the hoped-for arrival of 5,000 armed and trained Irgun cadres from Poland to bolster the 2,000-strong force in Palestine would go a long way to eroding the British Mandate in the face of an imminent cross-border conflagration in Europe. Britain could ill

> **BRITISH HISTORY MADE IN GERMANY**
>
> HESS PICKS A POINT FROM 1281
> Rudolf Hess, Hitler's deputy, delved into history for anti-British oratory yesterday. He was speaking at Komotau to employees of the Mannesmann steel tube works in connection with the Reichstag elections, which take place in Sudetenland on Sunday. Dealing with the Jews, he said: "Might I remind the British that their Government found it necessary to expel the Jews in 1281, confiscating all their property, and not merely 10 or 20 per cent?
>
> "They would longer be cheated by the Jews, who had become the scourge of the country. Reports of this period speak volumes. For 300 years England was without Jews, and did not fare so badly without them. On the contrary she became a flourishing country."
>
> BRITISH IN PALESTINE
> Becoming more up-to-date, he said that when a young man who could not be held responsible was hired as a murderer in Paris, sufficient consequences arose for the Jews in Germany.
>
> "They say that so many of these Jews are innocent. Were all the natives in Palestine guilty when all those houses were blown up by the British? Were all the Egyptians guilty who had to pay a high fine because a British High Commissioner was murdered?
>
> "Were the tens and thousands of poor women and children guilty whom the British shut up in their notorious camps in the Boer War? Were tens and thousands of Russians, who were murdered by the Cheka, or the women and children of Insurgent Spain, whose eyes were put out and ears cut off, all guilty?"
>
> Herr Hess emphasised necessity for 'sacrifices'. "We shall continue to make sacrifices for our safety through armaments, which have been forced upon us by others," he declared. "Germany has regained her equality with the other States, and no one will be able to tread upon her in the future. There is no Power in the world able to do it, even if the Churchills, Edens and Duff Coopers claim that it could be done with more armaments."
>
> *Dundee Courier*, Thursday, 1 December 1938

afford to have Palestine divert resources away from the more pressing European issues, so Whitehall might prefer to strike an early deal with the Zionists. In such an event, the Irgun would make for a loyal, trained ally for both frontline combat and to relieve British troops currently committed to the mandate. And the Arabs? They would be intimidated into acquiescence.

In Poland, Irgun emissary Avraham Stern, without recourse to the NZO, had been active in building a network of loyal militants such as future Israeli prime minister Menachem Begin, at the time commander of Betar. Contact with influential politicians was maintained and nurtured, allowing for the collection and shipment of arms to Palestine.

Back in Tel Aviv, Raziel briefed the first twenty Irgun volunteers to go for officer and NCO training courses in the Zakofna mountains of southwest Poland. Training would focus on sabotage and partisan warfare. When the course ended in May, Irgun operative Yaakov Meridor stayed behind to arrange for the packing and shipment of arms and ordnance to equip 5,000 Irgun fighters: French and Polish rifles, Hotchkiss machine guns, sidearms, grenades and explosives. Through all this, Jabotinsky remained oblivious of the major development to challenge the British administration in Palestine by force.

Irgun fighters undergoing pistol training. (Photo Jabotinsky Institute)

Of serious concern to Jabotinsky, though, was a marked deterioration in the Irgun–NZO relationship, which prompted him to call a meeting of all the factions to thrash out divergent issues. In February 1939, his impressive reputation preceding him, Raziel met with Jabotinsky in Paris. While NZO and Betar delegates expressed their thoughts on the best structure for the movement, Raziel's tacit persona left Jabotinsky both curious and impressed: an accomplished fighter with little to say, Hebrew-speaking, a devout Jew who prayed daily, well-read. It was therefore a simple matter to appoint Raziel as commander of the Palestine Betar, which effectively signalled the merging of the Irgun and Betar in the mandate. The Irgun's place in the Revisionist movement had been formalized, but on the ground, Raziel continued to operate as a virtual free agent.

At this precise time, it is also ironic that the British government launched the latest in a litany of initiatives on the future of Palestine. Convened at St James's Palace in London from 7 February to 17 March 1939, and presided over by Prime Minister Neville Chamberlain, Colonial Secretary Malcolm MacDonald had, prior to the conference, made it very clear that, in the event of no agreement being reached between the three affected parties, His Majesty's government would impose a solution on the Palestine débâcle.

Led by influential pan-Arab nationalist and politician, Jamal al-Husayni, the Palestinian Arabs position was unequivocal: end of the British Mandate, Palestinian independence, cessation of Jewish immigration, and no Jewish state in Palestine.

The Jewish delegates came from the Jewish Agency, orthodox Zionists and prominent British Jews. The Jewish Agency had ensured that the NZO was not invited. In fact, head of the Jewish Agency, David Ben-Gurion, who emerged as the principal Jewish decision-maker at the conference, had pushed for all Jewish delegates at the conference to fall under the umbrella of the Jewish Agency. The two main Jewish leaders, Chaim Weizmann and Ben-Gurion, had canvassed other Jewish delegates to accept the Peel recommendations as a framework for future negotiations. On this platform, the Jewish Agency tabled their position: the British Mandate to remain in place, no minority status for the Jews in Palestine, Jewish immigration to continue, dependent on Palestine's carrying capacity, and an injection of development capital.

Members of Jewish youth movements demonstrating in Tel Aviv against the British White Paper policy. (Photo Israel GPO)

As the month of February dragged on at St James, both Arab and Jewish delegates refused to bend in what they sought in Palestine. In separate meetings with the two parties, MacDonald's calls for compromise were stubbornly rejected. The Jewish Agency, in particular, found MacDonald's proposal of guaranteed minority status for Jews in an independent Palestine beyond contemplation, and ended their participation in any further formal discussions with the British.

On 27 February, the Tel Aviv-based daily newspaper *Davar* published a message from Ben-Gurion: "There is a scheme afoot to liquidate the National Home and turn us over to the rule of gang leaders." That same day, Palestine reacted to the news from London.

The *Sunderland Daily Echo and Shipping Gazette* on Monday, 27 February 1939, headlined, "Many Casualties in Palestine Terrorist Wave", "32 Arabs Killed and 50 Wounded" and "Tragedy Follows Day of Rejoicing".

Over the weekend, Palestinian Arabs held "demonstrations of rejoicing" at the news that an independent Arab Palestine, in which Jews would be a minority, was imminent. But on the Monday, in widespread, predominantly anti-Arab violence, thirty-two were killed and fifty wounded in fourteen separate and scattered bomb, landmine, and shooting incidents. In Haifa alone, twenty-four were killed and forty-four wounded in three bomb explosions in Arab areas. In Jerusalem's Old City market, three Arabs were killed and six wounded when a bomb exploded. In Tel Aviv a landmine exploded just after a train had passed.

With no apparent end to the self-perpetuating violence among the Arab, Jewish and British stakeholders in Palestine, on 17 May 1939 the British government again sought a solution to the dilemma by introducing a fresh tranche of political aims for Palestine, based on proposals at the failed London Conference. The latest White Paper, published as Parliamentary Document 6019, embodied three defining policies:

1. The objective of His Majesty's Government is the establishment within ten years of an independent Palestinian State in such treaty relations with the United Kingdom as will provide satisfactorily for the commercial and strategic requirements of both countries in the future.
2. No further Jewish immigration will be permitted unless the Arabs of Palestine are prepared to acquiesce in it.
3. There is now in certain areas no room for further transfers of Arab land, whilst in some other areas such transfers of land must be restricted if Arab cultivators are to maintain their existing standard of life and a considerable landless Arab population is not soon to be created.

The Revisionists viewed the White Paper with disdain and despair, especially the proposed restriction of Jewish immigration to no more than 30 percent of the total

L'POOL ZIONIST COUNCIL'S DISMAY

The Liverpool Zionist Central Council met last night to discuss the White Paper, and afterwards issued a statement including the following points:

"The Liverpool Jewish Community have been filled with the most profound dismay by the proposals contained in the White Paper on Palestine. The new policy is a betrayal of the pledges given to the Jewish people in 1917 and endorsed by every subsequent British Government. The historic connection between the Jewish people and Palestine, and their right to establish there a Jewish National Home, were formally recognised by 52 nations and embodied in the mandate by virtue of which Great Britain administers Palestine.

"The new policy will mean that loyalty is to be penalised and terrorism and revolt rewarded. The Jewish people refuse to accept this decision as the will of the British people.

"We as Jews and loyal British citizens will resist these proposals with every means in our power. In opposing this betrayal of a people who are suffering a persecution unparalleled in history and whose one hope lies in Palestine, we are confident that we will be supported by the great mass of democratic opinion in this country, and throughout the world."

A deputation of the leaders of the Jewish community in Liverpool is to be received by Merseyside M.P.s at the House of Commons on Monday afternoon.

Liverpool Evening Express, 18 May 1939

British soldiers on escort duty during the civil unrest, 1939. (Photo Israel GPO)

population. Palestinian Arabs rejected the British initiative for not going far enough, launching a fresh campaign of violence against the Yishuv to express their displeasure. Not for the first time, the whole moral and political issue of eye-for-an-eye retaliation against Arab terror dominated Zionist reaction. Jabotinsky left no doubt as to his position, tempered by exasperation:

> Each of us would wish that, in the event that it is essential to take action, it should be a direct reprisal against the murderers. But if a Jewish unit should dare to pursue an Arab gang, its members would be arrested and disarmed and they would be placed on trial—and many of them would be hung from the gallows. The choice does not lie between reacting against murderers or against the hostile public in general: the choice is between two practical possibilities—either reaction against the hostile public in general or general non-reaction.
>
> When we are speaking of war, we do not ask ourselves which is 'preferable'—to shoot or not to shoot. The sole question which may be asked in such cases is the reverse: which is 'worse', to be slaughtered or subjugated without resistance, or to resist with all the means at one's disposal, however cruel, because there is no 'preferable' in this case. Everything to do with war is 'bad', and the 'good' is non-existent. When you fire at foreign soldiers, do not lie to yourself and do not delude yourself that those you are shooting are the 'guilty'.
>
> If we were to begin to calculate what is preferable, then the reckoning would be very simple; if you wish to be 'good', then please allow yourself to be killed and renounce everything you hoped to defend: home, country, freedom, hope ...[*]

In the immediate wake of the release of the White Paper, the Irgun continued to respond on a like-for-like basis against the increased Arab attacks on the Jewish community. However, it would not be under Raziel's watch that anti-British operations would be incorporated into the movement's underground activities.

On 19 May 1939, the British police arrested Raziel at Lydda airport. He would only be released in 1941 when the British Army accepted his offer to act on their behalf to help overthrow the pro-Axis government in Iraq. On 20 May that year, while on operations in Iraq, Raziel was killed when the vehicle in which he was travelling was attacked by a Luftwaffe aircraft.

Irgun deputy commander, Hanoch (Strelitz) Kalai, was appointed commander-in-chief, and at his first meeting with his general headquarters staff, the decision was made to fight the British administration for the perfidy of the White Paper.

---

[*] Jabotinsky Institute.

British police block Allenby Street in Tel Aviv to prevent a mass protest against the British White Paper policy. (Photo Israel GPO)

The Lithuanian-born activist was a member of Betar and had served as a propaganda broadcaster for the Irgun radio station.

On Friday, 2 June, four bomb explosions rocked various parts of Jerusalem. A massive explosion at the Jaffa Gate Arab bus station, caused by a time bomb concealed in a petrol tin overnight, killed five Arabs and wounded nineteen. In the other three, more-controlled explosions, around 1,700 telephone lines were severed, including some used by the army and police.

On 9 June 1939, Irgun planned a bombing attack against Arab visitors to prisoners in the central jail in the Russian Compound in Jerusalem. The explosive device, hidden in a large basket of fruit and vegetables, would be conveyed by Rachel Ohevet-Ami (Habshush), a seventeen-year-old Jewish girl who spoke fluent Arabic on account of her family having emigrated from Yemen. Upon reaching the Russian Compound, her face veiled, Rachel asked an Arab boy to carry her basket. However, the weight of the basket aroused his suspicion. He approached a passing policeman and asked him to check the contents. Rachel was arrested immediately and a bomb-disposal expert detached the fuse and prevented the device from detonating. Appearing before a military tribunal Rachel Ohevet-Ami was sentenced to life imprisonment and taken to the women's prison in

Bethlehem, the first Jew to be incarcerated among Arab women prisoners. During the Second World War she was joined by other female members of the Irgun and Lehi. A string of appeals from various Jewish organizations would land on the desks of the British High Commissioner and the General Officer Commanding British forces in Palestine. One such combined petition from Jewish organizations not associated with the underground resistance, in September 1942 argued that

> the crime this girl has committed was a political one which can only be understood and judged in the connection with the political disturbances existing at that time as well as during the three years preceding the date of the offence ... It was quite clear from the circumstances that this girl had not acted alone but had been the instrument of other people whose instructions and direction she had carried out ... Similar disturbances had occurred in this country in 1929, and it is a fact that several members of this girl's family had been brutally done to death or horribly wounded in the 1929 riots.*

It would only be after the Second World War, seven years after her conviction, that Rachel was pardoned by the High Commissioner and released.

At 8.50 p.m. on the night of 11 June, two bombs exploded in letter boxes in Jerusalem's main post office, totally destroying the interior. The following morning, while sifting through the debris inside the building, British police constable Robert Clark was killed when the bomb he had discovered exploded. Elements of the Black Watch threw up a cordon around the city's Jewish quarter as the police conducted house-to-house searches.

During the night of 13/14 June, ten bombs exploded, destroying telephone booths and shop windows, while the railway station was "slightly damaged". A nightly curfew was immediately introduced in the town. Six days later, a powerful bomb exploded in Haifa's Arab vegetable market, killing eighteen and injuring twenty-four. Following demonstrations by angry Arab mobs, a curfew was imposed on the town. A curfew was also imposed on Jaffa after three bombs exploded on the 20th. There were no casualties.

On the 30th, fifteen Arabs were injured when a bomb exploded in a small wicker basket near an Arab café in Jerusalem's central business district. During a Palestine police stop-and-search operation instituted after gunmen shot and killed thirteen Arabs near Tel Aviv, fifty-three Zionist Revisionists were arrested for failing to provide proof of legal entry into Palestine. Reporting on the two incidents, the *Yorkshire Evening Post* said that the attacks were believed to be by "Jewish extremists".

---

* NZO Political Office, Jerusalem, correspondence on Rachel Habshush (Ohev Ami), life prisoner in Beit Lehem Prison.

A typical Arab fresh-produce market, this one in Safed, 1939. (Photo Israel GPO)

BOMB THAT FAILED TO EXPLODE UNDER CRICKET PAVILION

Match Resumed After Removal

Some 20 British residents in Haifa, including police officers, Iraq Petroleum Company officials, and their wives, narrowly escaped [death] on Sunday when a large bomb placed under the cricket ground pavilion failed to explode. It had been timed for five p.m., states the "Daily Telegraph and Morning Post" Jerusalem correspondent.

A match between the police and the company officials was in progress when the spectators heard a sizzling sound and saw smoke emerging from cracks in the floor of the pavilion. A party of the Royal Engineers, who were summoned, found a smoking fuse attached to a cylinder a foot high, weighing 40lb., filled with gelignite and rivets. The bomb failed to explode only because there was a slight defect in the fuse connection. After the removal of the bomb the match was resumed, the police winning by four wickets.

Ballymena Weekly Telegraph, Saturday, 12 August 1939

As punishment for these bombing incidents, on 5 July the British authorities imposed a collective fine of £1,000 on the Jewish quarter in northwest Jerusalem. In Haifa, the British military commander ordered "Jewish cafés and places of entertainment" to remain closed indefinitely.

Three Irgun-planted time bombs exploded in the Palestine broadcasting studios in Jerusalem during children's hour on 2 August: two in the control room and a third in one of the studios. Of the four wounded in the blasts, Mrs May Weissenberg, a South African English-language announcer and a Christian Arab employee died of their injuries the following day. Of particular concern to the authorities was that English children usually attended the broadcast in the studio, but on this day, none had arrived.

A week later, on 9 August, a bomb was thrown at a police post on picket duty outside the same studios. There were no casualties. Earlier that day, a time bomb exploded on board a new marine patrol boat, the *Sinbad II*, as it was cruising off Nathanya. A British policeman from London, Sergeant Geoffrey King, was killed and two British constables injured. After the boat sank, the two uninjured Palestine police crew members swam half a mile to shore, taking the two wounded constables with them.

One of the most active Irgun operatives was explosives expert Gundar 'Arieh' Yitzhaki, who is attributed with having thrown the first retaliatory explosive device into an Arab café in Yazur, a Palestinian town four miles east of Jaffa. He manufactured letter bombs that were mailed to Arabs in Jaffa and devised booby-trapped bombs that would explode when defusing attempts were made. He would, however, not be the first in history to meet his end in the pursuit of his high-risk occupation. On 5 August 1939, a bomb that he had just finished building in his workshop detonated in his hands. He died soon after British CID details arrived at the scene to investigate.

Two British police inspectors were killed on 26 August when a remote-detonated landmine exploded in Jerusalem. Ronald Barker, 31, from Reading, and Ralph Cairns, 31, from Preston, were on duty in the Jewish quarter of Jerusalem near the Jewish Agency when the landmine, believed to be of Jewish origin, was detonated by a person only thirty yards away. The military commander subsequently ordered the indefinite closure of all Jewish cinemas and cafés.

London had become encumbered with crisis upon crisis: the Irish Republican Army (IRA), Hitler and Palestine. On 16 January 1939, the IRA launched a two-year terror campaign of bombing and sabotage against the civil and military infrastructure of Britain, as five bombs exploded in London and three in Manchester. Codenamed the S-Plan or Sabotage Campaign, the IRA attacks during this period amounted to 300 explosions, ten deaths and ninety-six injuries.

Irgun: Revisionist Zionism 1931–1948

The inner yard of Kibbutz Gazit in the Lower Galilee, a typical kibbutz. (Zoltan Kluger/ GPO Israel)

In the second half of the 1930s, the now burgeoning armed forces of Nazi Germany remilitarized the Rhineland, annexed Austria, and took over the Sudetenland, Moravia and Bohemia. In London, expediency, compromise and tolerance dominated Prime Minister Chamberlain's dealings with Adolf Hitler, even to the extent of naïvely signing a worthless piece of German stationery purporting to reflect the desire of "our two peoples never to go to war with one another again". For those who did not regard Herr Hitler as a gentleman, Chamberlain's appeasement stood instead for duplicity and betrayal. The Treaty of Versailles now stood for nothing.

Despite Chamberlain's March 1939 assurance to the Commons that, in the event of a German invasion of Poland, "His Majesty's Government would feel themselves bound at once to lend the Polish Government all support in their power," Hitler would exploit London's timidity and belief in the efficacy of mediation, starting with the fabrication of Polish intransigence and belligerent rhetoric against alleged German interference in the internal affairs of the Free City of Danzig, thereby providing a justifiable reason to invade Poland itself.

In Palestine, Jew and Arab alike looked on attentively, in the knowledge that developments in Poland, with its 3.5 million Jews facing Hitler's abject hatred, would hold major ramifications for the Middle East.

3. TRUCE AND REVOLT

> I shall prove that the rulers of Britain actively helped the Nazis destroy the Jews of Europe. In the field of the destruction of the Jews, Britain was a confirmed 'collaborator' and cooperated with the Nazi murderers throughout all the years of the war.
>
> Irgun fighter Jehuda Lemberger during his trial before a British military court[*]

At precisely 4.45 a.m. on 1 September 1939, Hitler launched his invasion of Poland. In the air, the Luftwaffe claimed immediate air superiority, attacking airfields, the road and rail infrastructure, and industrial and administrative centres. On the ground, the highly mechanized Wehrmacht ploughed through the Polish countryside, with an astounding speed that soon became universally known as blitzkrieg. At 11.15 a.m. on 3 September, in a broadcast to the nation, Prime Minister Neville Chamberlain declared that "this country is at war with Germany".

In London, Palestine would now seldom be an item on the cabinet agenda. British policy on the mandate remained in place, the status of the White Paper in torpor. Any Jewish expectations of Britain softening in its handling of the mandate were in vain.

During a meeting of the Irgun general headquarters in Tel Aviv on 31 August, British intelligence officers and policemen burst in, arresting Raziel, Hanoch Kalai, Avraham Stern and Aharon Heichman. With the Irgun command in British cells when Hitler invaded Poland on 1 September 1939, Raziel firmly believed that it had now become essential to collaborate with the British against the common Nazi enemy. Accordingly, he simultaneously wrote to the British commander-in-chief in Palestine, to the mandatory government secretary and to the British police commissioner, informing them of his willingness to declare a truce, while offering to help the Allies fight the Germans. To coincide with this, Raziel, in the Sarafand camp, sent instructions to new Irgun commander, Polish-born Benyamin Zeroni, to go public with the suspension of Irgun operations. On 11 September, Zeroni, under protest, distributed a leaflet, which stated:

> To avoid disrupting the course of the war against Germany, and in order to invest maximum effort in assisting Great Britain and its allies, the Irgun Zvai

---
[*] Tavin & Alexander.

Jewish volunteers march in Tel Aviv in support of enlistment in the British army, 1940. (Photo Israel GPO)

Le'umi has decided to suspend all offensive activities in Palestine which could cause harm to the British government and in any way be of assistance to the greatest enemy the Jewish people has ever known—German Nazism.*

At the same time, Jabotinsky declared full NZO—and therefore the Revisionists'—support for Britain's war against Nazi Germany. Shortly afterwards, Yaakov Meridor returned from Poland to take over command of the Irgun from Zeroni. Meridor's first priority was to break Raziel and the Irgun leadership out of prison. While succeeding in making his way into Sarafand dressed as a labourer, the escape plan was however aborted.

Meanwhile, Meridor had discovered that a divergence of opinion had developed between the Irgun HQ staff and Raziel over the latter's failure to secure favourable conditions in exchange for collaboration with the British. On the outside, NZO leader Dr Aryeh Altman, who himself was under house arrest, lobbied the administration for the release of the prisoners now that the Revisionists had declared their loyalty to Britain's war effort.

Despite the Nazis swift subjugation of Poland, and with the nightmare of the Holocaust yet to materialize, the resourcefulness and good fortune of many

---

* www.etzel.org.il

Revisionists and other militant Zionist activists in Poland saw them flee the Nazis and sneak their way into Palestine. But in October 1939, the Irgun was rudderless, with its leadership in captivity at each other's throats over disparate Irgun policies toward the British administration in Palestine.

Towards the end of the month, a manacled Raziel was brought to the King David Hotel in Jerusalem to meet with the mandate's deputy inspector general and head of the Criminal Investigation Department (CID), Arthur Giles, the deputy government secretary and a respected leader of the Yishuv, Pinhas Rutenberg. The next day, Raziel was released conditionally, but despite his demands for the release of all Irgun members incarcerated by the British, it would be eight months before Raziel's comrades were released.

Soon after their release, a heated meeting took place at the Irgun's general HQ in Tel Aviv, highlighted by an acrimonious confrontation between David Raziel and Avraham Stern. Stern argued that the Irgun was being hamstrung by the Revisionist Party and should be allowed to independently determine its own agenda and political destiny. Raziel, however, was adamant that the Irgun would not survive without the Revisionists, as the party not only secured its funding, but was also the Irgun's main pool for recruits.

PALESTINE DEFENCE

JEWS' VOLUNTARY TAX ON INCOME
Thousands Join National Service Campaign

Measures to be taken by the Jews for the defence of Palestine are announced to-day. They include:—
A special voluntary tax for defence of up to one-fifth of their income;
Volunteering for national service in co-operation with the British Army.
The Jewish National Assembly of Palestine, meeting in Jerusalem, had asked all Jews in the country, in view of the present emergency, to give a part of their income. Money raised will be devoted to the conservation of the economy of Palestine, to the stimulation of home agriculture and industry, and to vital works in connection with the general requirements of defence in the Near East.
It is also stated that 135,900 Jews have become national service volunteers. They will be divided into two categories, men between 18 and 35 for military service and men between 35 and 50 to be trained in A.R.P. and other reserve duties. The 35,000 Jewish women who have volunteered will be responsible for first aid and ambulance duties.

Birmingham Mail, Thursday, 5 October 1939

Irgun: Revisionist Zionism 1931–1948

The arrival in Palestine of British Secretary of State for War Anthony Eden, seen here in an open car with Brigadier-General Allan, 1940. (Photo Eric and Edith Matson Collection)

The issue of the truce was equally contentious. Regardless of Britain being fully engaged in a global conflict, Stern contended that the fight against the British had to continue for as long as they ruled Palestine. Raziel, however, and in agreement with Jabotinsky, saw Nazi Germany as the prime foe, the common enemy, and therefore the Zionist activists in Palestine should not in any way hinder Britain's war effort. Personality differences notwithstanding, the inevitable split occurred on 17 July 1940.

Stern broke away to form an organization initially know as *Irgun Zvai Le'umi Be'yisrael*, the National Military Organization in Israel. Raziel's organization remained titled the *Irgun Zvai Leumi Be'eretz Yisrael*, the National Military Organization in Eretz Israel. Later, Stern's organization became known as *Lohamei Herut Yisrael* (Israel Freedom Fighters), or Lehi for short. They were commonly also referred to as the Stern Gang. A much-weakened, split Irgun was now vulnerable to verbal attacks from the Haganah and easier scrutiny by the British CID.

At the time of the crisis within the Jewish resistance movement in Palestine, Jabotinsky had been in the US actively building support for a Jewish army in Palestine. While visiting a Betar camp near New York on 4 August 1940, Ze'ev Jabotinsky MBE, founder of the Revisionist-Zionism movement and its youth wing, Betar, and erstwhile Irgun commander, died of a heart attack, aged fifty-nine.

His paper, *Instead of Excessive Apology, 1911*, which he wrote in Russian, included a passage which epitomizes his mantra as a Zionist activist:

> Our habit of constantly and zealously answering to any rabble has already done us a lot of harm and will do much more ... We do not have to apologize for anything. We are a people as all other peoples; we do not have any intentions to be better than the rest. As one of the first conditions for equality we demand the right to have our own villains, exactly as other people have them ... We do not have to account to anybody, we are not to sit for anybody's examination and nobody is old enough to call on us to answer. We came before them and will leave after them. We are what we are, we are good for ourselves, we will not change, nor do we want to.[*]

In Tel Aviv, the Irgun's new-look general HQ set about patching up the hiatus caused by the split. Having enlisted in the Irgun in 1939, Russian-born Yitzhak Berman, together with fellow member Aryeh Posek, concentrated efforts on establishing close working ties with British Army intelligence.

In 1941, Berman enlisted in the British Army, serving in intelligence. By this time, Rommel's Afrika Korps was striking ever eastward towards Egypt, while in the Levant, the French Vichy government was occupying Syria and Lebanon on behalf of Berlin. In Iraq, Rashid Ali al Kilani had started a revolt, taking over strategic oilfields and holding British embassy staff hostage. In Cairo, army intelligence approached Berman to see if he could arrange for elements of the Irgun to blow up the refineries in Baghdad. A four-man Irgun team, commanded by Raziel and comprising Yaakov Meridor, Yaakov Sika-Aharoni and Yaakov Harazi, was put together. From the military airfield at Tel Nof, an RAF transport flew the unit to Habaniyeh where, upon their arrival, their orders were changed: they were to conduct reconnaissance missions ahead of a planned capture of the town of Fallujah, thirty-seven miles west of Baghdad.

On 20 May, a British major and his aide took the Irgun men into the target area, where Meridor and Sika-Aharoni crossed a river in a boat, while the rest of the team drove back to base. On their way, a German aircraft scored a direct hit on the car, instantly killing Raziel and the British officer.

Once more, cracks started to appear in the now grieving Irgun command structure. Yaakov Meridor succeeded Raziel, but it would be more than a year later before the Irgun recovered from the devastating blow of their commander's death.

As the war entered 1943, it was clear that the Allies' fortunes were starting to turn in their favour. But in Palestine, the magnitude of the Holocaust was becoming known. Jewish immigrant ships were not only blocked from entering Palestine, but were on occasion forced to make the return voyage to Europe. The Irgun command was now under pressure, particularly from its younger members, to terminate the truce with the mandatory power it had declared when the war commenced. Senior

---

[*] Kai Bird, *Crossing Mandelbaum Gate: Coming of Age Between the Arabs and Israelis, 1956–1978* (Simon & Schuster, New York, 2010).

Irgun: Revisionist Zionism 1931–1948

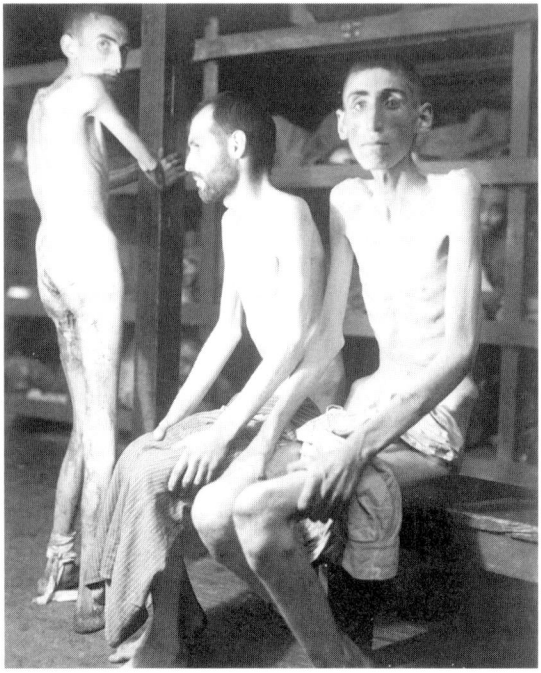

The plight of Jews in the Nazi concentration camps. (Photo NARA)

Irgun commander Eliyahu Lankin insisted that the Irgun should find a new commander who had no connection with the events of the Stern split. Meridor, accepting that his leadership role could only ever have been transient, concurred, and the Irgun command looked at the recently arrived Menachem Begin.

Born in Belorussia (Belarus), his father an ardent Zionist, the young Begin joined Betar at the age of sixteen. While reading law at the University of Warsaw, he organized a Jewish self-defence group to counter anti-Semitism on campus. Graduating in 1935, he became an adherent of Jabotinsky's Revisionist Zionism. Two years later, his meteoric rise through the ranks saw him become head of the Betar in Czechoslovakia, and thereafter the leader of the movement's largest branch, that of Poland.

With the German invasion of Poland in 1939, Begin fled to Vilnius with other Jewish leaders to escape inevitable arrest. In September the following year, Begin was arrested by the Soviet People's Commissariat for Internal Affairs, NKVD, for his pre-war Zionist activities. Incarcerated in Vilnius's notorious Lukiškės Prison, Begin was deprived of sleep when interrogated night after night. Before being sent to the Pechora labour camps in June 1941, Begin spent seven days in solitary confinement:

> Having only three and a half paces within which to move my body in that triangular, windowless, smelly cell, I had to make up for it with mental exercise. Those 170 hours were not very pleasant. I was given nothing to eat but dry bread and water. But there were worse things. There was dirt in very large quantities. The sanitary pail was never taken out. There was a bare stone floor. For a pillow I had to use my arm—a rather small, hard and painful pillow. By day it was too hot, and at night freezing cold. In addition I was entertained by a thriving colony of rats. But, I survived it.*

---

* Menachem Begin, *The Revolt: The Warrior Years of Israel's Brilliant Architect of Peace* (Dell Publishing, New York, 1977).

Following Begin's release in terms of the Sikorski–Mayski Agreement between the Soviet Union and Poland, in July 1941 he enlisted with the Free Polish Army as an officer cadet. He arrived in Palestine with the Polish Army in May 1942, where he elected, with many other Jews, to stay in Palestine and join the fight for an independent Jewish state. Granted a "leave of absence without an expiration" by Polish general Michał Karaszewicz-Tokarzewski, Begin joined the Irgun in December 1942. He would lose both his parents and his brother Herzl in the Holocaust.

Exactly a year later, Begin was appointed to head the Irgun high command—General Headquarters—the supreme body, also including Yaakov Meridor, Aryeh Ben-Eliezer, Eliyahu Lankin and Shlomo Lev-Ami (Levi). Lev-Ami was the only survivor from the previous high command.

Menachem Begin as a young Betar movement leader in Warsaw. (Photo Jabotinsky Institute)

On 1 February 1944, Begin led the Irgun in a proclamation of revolt:

Sons of Israel, Hebrew youth!
We stand at the final stage of the war, we face an historic decision on our future destiny.
The truce proclaimed when war broke out has been violated by the British authorities. The rulers of the country have taken into account neither loyalty nor concessions nor sacrifice; they have continued to implement their aim: the liquidation of sovereign Zionism.
We must draw the necessary conclusions without wavering. There can no longer be a truce between the Hebrew nation and youth and the British administration of Eretz Israel, which is betraying our brethren to Hitler. Our nation will fight this regime, fight to the end.
And this is our demand:
Rule over Eretz Israel must immediately be handed over to a provisional Hebrew government.

Despite the Irgun's 'truce', the British army in Palestine remained ever vigilant during the war. (Photo Sergeant Desmond Davis)

The Hebrew government of Eretz Israel, the sole legal representative of the Jewish people, must, immediately after its establishment, begin the implementation of the following principles:
a. establish a national Hebrew army.
b. conduct negotiations with all authorized bodies on the organization of the mass evacuation of European Jewry to Eretz Israel.*

By 1944, the Irgun leadership had become disillusioned as the immigration deadline provided in the 1939 White Paper approached. As the Jewish position in east and central Europe deteriorated rapidly in the last period of a fragile peace, the British Mandate administration had imposed severe restrictions on Jewish immigration into Palestine. At a time when Nazi genocide was systematically annihilating the Jewish race in continental Europe, Palestine could provide a haven of refuge from Hitler's vision of a Jewish-free world. For the Irgun, violence was the only means to force the mandatory power to lift its restrictive immigration policy.

Although the Irgun was initially intended to be the military arm of the Revisionist movement, it had rapidly evolved into an independent entity removed from the latter's control. However, the Revisionists remained the Irgun's almost exclusive source of recruits, with the Revisionist youth movement, Betar, providing pre-military

---

* www.etzel.org.il

HIDE VICTIMS OF HITLER

Daily Herald Reporter Washington

President Roosevelt to-night called on every German and everyone under Nazi domination to show he did not share Hitler's "insane criminal desires" by helping the persecuted.

"Let him hide these pursued victims, help them to get over their borders and do what he can to save them from the Nazi hangman," he said. "I ask him also to keep watch and record evidence that will one day be used to convict the guilty."

Mr. Roosevelt also called on the free peoples of Europe and Asia to open their frontiers temporarily to the victims of oppression. He marked the importance of the occasion by reading out a formal statement at his Press conference. He listed the atrocities by Germans and Japanese and went on: "As the result of events of the last few days, hundreds of thousands of Jews who had found a haven from death in Hungary and the Balkans, are now threatened with annihilation.

"Eve of Triumph"

"That these innocent people who have already survived a decade of Hitler's fury should perish on the very eve of triumph over the barbarism which their persecution symbolises would be major tragedy. It is therefore fitting that we should again proclaim our determination that none who participate in these acts of savagery shall go unpunished. That warning applies not only to the leaders. All who knowingly take part in the deportation of Jews to their death in Poland, or Norwegians and French to their death in Germany are equally guilty with the executioner. Insofar as the necessity of military operations permits, this Government will use all means at its command to aid the escape of all intended victims of the Nazi and Jap executioner regardless of race or religion or colour."

* The British Government associates itself wholeheartedly with the declaration by President Roosevelt, it was stated in London last night, and emphasises its determination to co-operate in helping and giving refuge to those who escape Nazi or Nazi-inspired tyranny.

training for potential Irgun members. Furthermore, Irgun members were able to mask their affiliation with the underground paramilitary movement by assuming active roles in both the Revisionist Party and Betar.

Jewish volunteers of the Second World War Auxiliary Territorial Service in Palestine. (Photo Zoltan Kluger)

In such manner, Jabotinsky, as head of the Betar immigration department from 1938 to 1940, had been able to direct the Irgun's organization of illegal immigration into Palestine. The exact number of illicit entrants into Palestine had been difficult to establish, but from May 1939 to 1944 the British administration registered close to twenty thousand. Most migrants had arrived before 1941, after which the British had significantly tightened military-civilian frontier controls. Official American intelligence sources estimated that some 50,000 illegal Jewish immigrants had arrived in Palestine in the period 1937 to 1944. With units in Poland and other European countries, and supported by 'humanitarian' funding from the US and elsewhere, the Irgun was responsible for a significant proportion of this figure.

Early in 1944, Britain was warned that the 'armistice' declared by the Irgun at the beginning of the war had been disregarded by the British government and had, therefore, been terminated. On this basis, the Irgun recommenced its campaign of violence against the British, with a view to intimidating London into revoking the white paper.

When the revolt was launched, in addition to the regional commands, Begin and his HQ staff divided the Irgun's 'combat' structure into four sections:

1. Army of the Revolution (AR)
2. Shock Units (SU)
3. Assault Force (AF)
4. Revolutionary Propaganda Force (RPF)*

The AR was, in reality, only a section on paper. Intended as a reserve pool for the other three sections, the section never had any officers and trained cadres were immediately posted to the three active sections.

The title of Shock Units was simply a formalization of what had already been in existence: the 'Red Section' or the 'Black Squad'. Originally the brainchild of Yaakov Meridor, the Red Section was solely dedicated to clandestine operations, in what Begin described as "an underground within an underground", or in today's military parlance, 'special forces'. The section's operators were specially selected for their dark-skinned Arabic appearance and fluency in the language. With the secrecy of the real identity of the operators an absolute imperative, only a select few knew of the existence of the Red Section, its ranks filled by loyal Irgun members who had 'deserted' from the movement with much open condemnation of the Irgun. The complexion of the SU reflected the ethnic diversity of the Jewish diaspora and the Yishuv: Tunisian, Polish, British, Argentinian, South African, American, French, Belgian, Iraqi, Czech, Syrian.

At the commencement of the revolt, the SU continued to act in the manner of its predecessor, but as the fight for an independent homeland intensified, the SU merged with the Assault Force (AF) to form the principal fighting arm of the Irgun. The AF continued to enjoy almost total autonomy, which did not always sit well with the Irgun's regional commanders or the intelligence services in the Revolutionary Propaganda Force (RPF).

The RPF was the tool used by the Irgun to disseminate the 'message of the revolt', giving explanations of the actions of the Irgun, while countering regional and global hate propaganda.

Arguably, for the Irgun the RPF's greatest psychological victory was at the Western or Wailing Wall in Jerusalem. Known in Islam as the sacred Buraq Wall, the small section of stone wall of the ancient Second Jewish Temple begun by Herod the Great is the holiest shrine where Jews are permitted to pray. In 1929, a British order-in-council decreed that, because Muslims were the sole legitimate owners of the Wailing Wall, Jews would be forbidden to blow the ceremonial horn, the Shofar, at the site.

On Yom Kippur, or Day of Atonement, the holiest day in the Jewish calendar, at sunset on the 'Sabbath of Sabbaths', the Shofar would be blown to mark the end of the fast. In 1943, according to Begin's eyewitness account, there was a strong presence of British police "armed with rifles and batons" at the Wailing Wall to prevent the

---

* Begin.

British army stop-and-search operations of Jewish bus passengers. (Photo Sergeant Desmond Davis)

"illegal act" of the blowing of the Shofar from happening. Possibly more as a symbol of defiance, the Shofar sounded, resulting in an "unrestrained" response from the police who took to the crowd with their batons. The ignominy prompted Begin to declare: "What the Roman proconsuls did not dare do, Britain's Commissioners are doing," promising that "when the time came we would cleanse our people of this shame, and if we should have the strength we would not permit the oppressors myrmidons to violate our Holy Place, disturb our prayers and desecrate our festival."

The following year, the RPF launched a sustained campaign, warning the British authorities in no uncertain terms not to interfere in way with that year's Day of Atonement religious activities at the Wailing Wall. On consecutive nights, Irgun operators, given the sobriquet 'pasters-up', ensured that the message was indelibly placed in the public domain:

1. On the Day of Atonement, at the Western Wall, large numbers of people will unite with the spirit of the martyrs of Israel who fell victim to German cruelty and British treachery.

2. The principles of civilized humanity dictate that the sacred prayer should not be disturbed, nor the Holy Place violated.
3. The British Government—ruling temporarily against the will of the Jewish people in its Homeland—is required not to infringe these principles.
4. Any British policeman who on the Day of the Atonement dares to burst into the area of the Wailing Wall and to disturb the traditional service will be regarded as a criminal and will be punished accordingly.[*]

For the first time in fourteen years, the British police were noticeable by their absence from the Wailing Wall on the Day of Atonement. The "trumpet of revolt", the Shofar, was freely blown.

The Assault Force was the Irgun's "messenger", the vanguard of underground resistance "to disintegrate alien rule". Heavily defended British administrative buildings and army barracks would be infiltrated and bombed. The road and rail network infrastructure, including bridges, would be mined and sabotaged. The only day of respite for the British from the Irgun's hit-and-run acts of terror was the Jewish Sabbath, a tradition started by the devout Zionist David Raziel.

From February 1944, the Irgun conducted periodic raids on British Mandate buildings, with an emphasis on the use of landmines and bombs to destroy property. While efforts were made to avoid bloodshed, it was inevitable that British, Jewish and Arab police and auxiliaries would fall victim to the Irgun's fresh campaign of violence. The Irgun would distribute illegal broadsheets to claim responsibility for the attacks.

On 12 February, the offices of the Palestine department of migration in Jerusalem, Tel Aviv and Haifa were partially destroyed by bombs. There had been reports of seven explosions and the discovery afterwards of three unexploded mines. There were no casualties.

During the night of 26/27 February, the government tax offices in the same three cities were blown up with landmines, again with no casualties.

On the night of 23 March, the headquarters of the police and CID in Jerusalem, Jaffa and Haifa were seriously damaged by explosive devices. Six British police officers were killed and a number of others seriously wounded. In the raid, led by Irgun commander of the Fighting Force in Jerusalem, Rahamim Cohen, the police HQ in the centre of the city was seriously damaged, while windows within a radius of 200 yards shattered. In an exchange of fire with a policeman, one of the Irgun fighters, Asher Benziman (Avshalom) was fatally wounded.

A wing of the district police HQ and British intelligence in Jaffa blew up just after the building had been evacuated following the discovery of four sacks containing

---
[*] Ibid.

Irgun: Revisionist Zionism 1931–1948

Irgun bomb damage to the British police HQ in Jerusalem. (Photo Matson Photographic Services)

thirty sticks of gelignite in an air-raid shelter under the building. An Irgun unit, led by Amichai Paglin, was responsible. At the CID HQ in Haifa, British constables James Mackie, Arthur Harding and William Allison were killed when a landmine, planted by an Irgun unit commanded by Yaakov Hillel, exploded in the building at 11.30 p.m. Together with several injured policemen, the casualties occurred in a billet on the third floor.

On that same night, there were three separate shooting incidents in the crowded streets of Tel Aviv, resulting in the deaths of British constable Douglas Caley and Charles Brown, the chief clerk at district police HQ in Jaffa.

An official statement released by the British authorities stated that a number of persons, dressed in British police uniforms, had gained entrance to police HQ in Jerusalem by using a ladder. On discovering the intruders, Assistant Superintendent John Scott opened fire, but was himself fatally wounded. A Jewish man, arrested nearby, was found in possession of a bomb and some ammunition, while another was arrested at Rachel's tomb, near Bethlehem, in possession of an automatic pistol and twenty-four rounds of ammunition.

Two days later, the British administration reintroduced the death sentence in Palestine for offences which since 1940 had been punishable only by life imprisonment. They include the discharge of firearms, depositing of bombs and explosives,

Truce and Revolt

A British soldier displays grenades discovered in a Tel Aviv school, during a sweep to round up suspected members of Jewish underground organizations. (Photo Sergeant Turner)

carrying firearms, ammunition or bombs, and interference with or damage to transport, water, electricity, or telephone services.

A 5 p.m. to 5 a.m. curfew was imposed in the municipal area of Tel Aviv and the Jewish quarter of Haifa.

The Palestine Broadcasting Service station at Ramallah was seized on the night of 18 May. Attempts to use the station failed, but some equipment was damaged in the raid.

Early in the morning of 14 July, a building housing the government land registry offices and the Jerusalem district police was demolished, destroying irreplaceable files and causing several casualties.

The Jaffa divisional police HQ and two police stations on the Jaffa–Tel Aviv boundaries were attacked with bombs and gunfire on the night of 22 August, inflicting several casualties.

On the night of 27 September, attacks were carried out on the police stations at Bayt Dajan, Qalqilya, Qatrah and the eastern station in Haifa. There were several casualties.

The liberal Zionist press and Yishuv leaders in Palestine were unreserved in their condemnation of the Irgun's terror activities. An editorial in the *ha-Ares* of 15 February, claiming to express the sentiments of the vast majority of the Palestine Jewish community, accused the perpetrators of the bombings of the migration department

PALESTINE TERRORISTS WARNED

Criminals Who Are Impeding The War Effort
Mr. J. V. W. Shaw, officer administrating the Government of Palestine, and General Sir Bernard Paget (Commander-in-Chief, Middle East Forces) yesterday issued a statement impressing upon the public, especially the Jewish public, the seriousness of the situation created by terrorist outrages in Palestine. The statement declared:

"Palestine, through the exertions and sacrifices of his Majesty's Forces and the forces of the Allies, has enjoyed for five years virtual immunity from the horrors of war which have caused such unspeakable suffering elsewhere.

"Since early in the present era Palestine has, however, been the scene of a series of outrages—crimes of violence by Jewish terrorists acting with the deliberate intention of bringing about by force developments favourable to the realisation of political aims.

"Officers and men of the security services have been murdered in cold blood and shot while doing their duty in the defence of life and property, innocent passers-by have been killed. Government buildings to the value of scores of thousands of pounds have been destroyed by explosives and fire. An attempt, providentially unsuccessful, was made to assassinate his Majesty's representative in ambush.

"This Evil Thing"
"Mr. Shaw, officer administering the Government of Palestine, and General Sir Bernard Paget (Commanding-in-Chief, Middle East Forces) call upon the Jewish community as a whole to do their utmost to assist the forces of law and order in eradicating this evil thing within their midst. Verbal condemnation of outrages on the platform and in the Press may have its effect, but is not in itself enough. What is required is actual collaboration with the forces of law and order, especially the giving of information leading to the apprehension of assassins and their accomplices.

"Accordingly, his Excellency and the Commander-in-Chief now call upon the Jewish community in Palestine, their leaders and representative bodies, to recognise and discharge their responsibilities and not to allow the good name of the Yishuv to be prejudiced by acts which can only bring shame and dishonour on the Jewish people as a whole."

Truce and Revolt

> Small Body of Extremists
> Colonel Stanley (Colonial Secretary), after describing recent terrorist outrages in Palestine in the House of Commons, yesterday, said that these attacks were the work of a relatively small body of extremists and were condemned by the responsible leaders of Jewry in Palestine and throughout the world. Undoubtedly a certain number of arms had either been stolen from, or in some cases sold by, troops.
>
> *Birmingham Daily Post*, Thursday, 12 October 1944

offices of harming the cause of the Jewish people at a time when important decisions about Zionism were awaited from the British and the Americans. The Jewish community was urged to exert greater efforts to curb the terrorism, and eliminate those terrorists who are prepared to "bridge over all too lightly the gap between political debates and murder".

A Jewish pedestrian is searched by British policemen in the authorities' ongoing drive to apprehend underground fighters. (Photo Israel GPO)

A Jewish woman is helped aboard a British army lorry during a sweep in Tel Aviv for members of Jewish terrorist organizations. (Sgt W. R. H. Turner/ No 1 Army Film & Photographic Unit via IWM)

Following the destruction of the land registry offices in Jerusalem, the *Palestine Post*, the largest Zionist daily newspaper, commented on 18 July: "For the misguided criminals there is nothing but public condemnation. They are young fanatics, crazed by the sufferings of their people into believing that destruction will bring healing."

When the affiliation between the Irgun and the American-based Hebrew Committee of National Liberation (HCNL) surfaced in Palestine, in the 22 May 1944 edition of *HaMishmar*, the daily organ of the Socialist-Zionist, secular Jewish youth movement *HaShomer HaTzair* (The Young Guard) attacked the Irgun's activities, accusing the organization of portraying "all the ugly symptoms of fascism":

> In Palestine, Irgun members have been killing British and Jewish police from ambush, in order to drive out the conquerors. In the US, they have helped to defer the solution of the political problems in Palestine. The terrorist acts in Palestine and the HCNL mockery in the US were dangerous symptoms of a malignant disease. The only remedy is to do everything conceivable to isolate the Irgun and the movement which produced it—Revisionism.

Kol Tsion HaLokhemet, the 'Voice of Fighting Zion', the underground radio station of the Irgun since 1939, was damning in an immediate post-war indictment of the British Mandate: "What the German Nazis did to our brothers in Europe the British Nazis shall not do to us. We shall fight them as fiercely as freedom loving people have always fought tyranny. We shall not be enslaved."*

---

*   Tavin & Alexander.

4. SMITE THE ENEMY HARD

> Very possibly Nazi-Britain will, in a few weeks' time, crown herself, with the aid of her Washingtonian partners, the representative of Civilisation and the executor of the United Nations will in Eretz Israel. But the comedy will not avail her. It will end in great tragedy, particularly for those who act it out for the whole world to see and at the expense of a fighting and bleeding nation. Nazi-Britain will not rule in our country. Any attempt to extend or renew a regime of occupation in our country, under one guise or another will bring on such an offensive against the oppressors as has not yet been seen during all the years of our fight for the liberation of our country.
>
> Irgun communiqué 11 April 1948*

By September 1944, the resistance activities of the Irgun had become increasingly annoying and embarrassing to the official leadership of the Yishuv, the Jewish Agency. At two meetings between Begin and the Haganah command, head of the Haganah General HQ, Moshe Sneh, warned that a continuation of the Irgun's military campaign would result in a clash between the Irgun and the legitimately elected representatives of the Jews in Palestine. Haganah leader Eliyahu Golomb was succinct in his contribution: the Yishuv would resort to force to destroy the Irgun.

However, Begin retained a conciliatory tone, assuring the Haganah leaders that the Irgun did not aspire to assuming control of the Yishuv, but merely existed as an essential but transient mechanism to maintain pressure on Britain to heed the desires of Zionism. However, an event in Egypt in November that year abruptly ended any possible thoughts of a united liberation front between the Haganah and the Irgun.

Since his breakaway from the Irgun, the charismatic and radical Avraham Stern with his Lehi organization waged his own campaign of terror against the British authorities in Palestine. Continually on the move to avoid capture by the CID, Stern became one of the most wanted people in Palestine, his 'revolutionary' bank robberies earning him a reputation among the Jewish Agency and the Irgun of a criminal on a personal crusade. Stern was eventually shot and killed on 12 February 1942 while being arrested by the British police in a safe house in Tel Aviv. But his legacy fuelled the Lehi's revolutionary cause, especially in the person of the new Lehi leader and former Irgun member, Yitzhak Shamir.

---

* Ibid.

Irgun: Revisionist Zionism 1931–1948

The military funeral procession in Cairo for Lord Moyne, the British Resident Minister in the Middle East. (Photo Sergeant A. Drennan)

Born Walter Edward Guinness in Ireland, Lord Moyne had served for a year as Churchill's Secretary of State for the Colonies, before taking up a post as Deputy Resident Minister of State in Cairo from August 1942. Appointed British Resident Minister of the Middle East in January 1944, Lord Moyne was perceived by Shamir to be anti-Semitic and racist, responsible for the mass murder of Hungarian Jews. His death in the name of the liberation would internationalize the Palestine Mandate issue. It would also show the British and the Arab world that the agents of Revisionist Zionism could strike at Britain at will.

On 6 November 1944, two Lehi members personally selected by Shamir, Beirut-born Eliyahu Hakim and *sabra** Eliyahu Bet-Zuri, shot Lord Moyne as he arrived at his Cairo home for lunch. He succumbed to his wounds in hospital that evening. Hakim and Bet-Zuri were arrested shortly afterwards, would stand trial and be convicted in an Egyptian court, and be hanged on 23 March 1945.

Shocked at the loss of a personal friend and a political ally, Churchill's condemnation of those responsible cast an accusing shadow over the whole Zionist movement's quest for a homeland:

> ... this shameful crime which has shocked the world. It has affected none more strongly than those, like myself, who, in the past, have been the consistent

---

* A Jew born in the mandate, and later, Israeli territory. From *sabra*, a local prickly pear.

friends of the Jews and constant architects of their future ... If our dreams for Zionism are to end in the smoke of the assassin's pistol, and our labours for its future produce only a new set of gangsters worthy of Nazi Germany, many, like myself, will have to reconsider the position we have maintained so consistently and so long in the past ... these wicked activities must cease, and those responsible for them must be destroyed root and branch.

Nottingham Evening Post, Friday, 17 November 1944

There was simultaneous condemnation from a hastily convened Jewish Agency executive, which declared a "Hunting Season" against "terrorist organizations" in the Palestine Mandate. In a damning indictment of the two militant Revisionist organizations, the executive called for the "traitors" to be "isolated and abandoned ... until terror ceases and its organization is eradicated". In direct Biblical references, the body admonished the Yishuv to "root out the evil from thy midst" and "the men of the city shall stone him with stones".

In response, the Irgun's RPF produced a leaflet appealing to "loyal Jews" for calm, while attacking Ben-Gurion "who has profaned his lips with the hysterical cry: blood for blood, and eye for an eye!" For the common good of the revolt, Begin knew that they could ill-afford to draw the Haganah into what he referred to as "fraternal strife".

Working in close collaboration with British intelligence and British police, the Haganah's intelligence wing, Shai (*Sherut Yediot*), commenced the systematic gathering of information on Irgun and Lehi members. Some 250 members of the elite Haganah mobile fighting unit, Palmach (*Plugot Hamahatz*), were issued with lists of names and deployed in operations to shadow and kidnap Irgun fighters. They also provided a personal protection service to leaders of the Jewish Agency in anticipation of Irgun and Lehi reprisals.

Nearly a thousand underground suspects were handed over to the British authorities, based on lists of names prepared by Shai. From the High Commissioner in Jerusalem, the colonial offices in London had, however, been made aware that the Jewish Agency's anti-terrorist campaign was also being exploited to remove Revisionist Party members from the political arena in Palestine by handing them over to the British.

The Palmach's most significant capture took place on 27 February 1945 when Polish-born Yaakov Tavin (born Farshtei), the Irgun's head of their intelligence service, Delek, was kidnapped and held captive at Kibbutz Ein Harod for six months, where he was severely tortured.

Ironically, this brought immediate condemnation from the supreme Jewish religious governing body in the Yishuv, the Chief Rabbinate, referring to the work of the Palmach as lawless "Ku Klux Klan acts". This public announcement fuelled an ever-growing lobby within the Yishuv against the Haganah's vendetta against fellow

British soldiers arrest two suspected underground fighters.

countrymen. By the end of the British Mandate, some 440 terrorist suspects had been transported to internment camps in Eritrea, the Sudan and Kenya.

Towards the spring of 1945, and as a sense of Allied victory in Europe was being felt, the Irgun started to recover from the Haganah's cleansing exercise. In May, there were fresh incidents of sabotage. Homemade mortars had also been placed opposite British targets, including the King David Hotel (accommodating the British military HQ and the mandate secretariat) and the government printers in Jerusalem, and the Sarona military camp in Tel Aviv.

With the return to peace in Europe, in July 1945 the British electorate put Clement Atlee's Labour Party into power. In Palestine, the Yishuv leadership viewed the change in Westminster with measured optimism, based on Labour's election canvassing pledge that the much-despised White Paper would be revoked, Holocaust survivors would be allowed to immigrate to Palestine, and progress would be made towards a Jewish homeland. However, in the euphoria of a landslide victory at the polls, Atlee's new administration reneged on all these promises. In *The Revolt*, Begin writes:

[British Foreign Secretary Ernest] Bevin opened his mouth; and the world tumbled about the ears of the credulous. That Midsummer Night's Dream vanished. No Labour promise, no Blackpool resolution, no friendship. All that remained was the traditional British fist, and facing us was Bevin whose dislike for the Jews was already legend.*

At Haganah HQ on 23 September, a disillusioned Moshe Sneh sent a telegram to Jewish Agency executive chairman David Ben-Gurion suggesting the staging of a "grave incident" as a warning to Britain of the serious consequences of failing to honour their promises. Within days, Ben-Gurion responded, fully concurring with Sneh and advocating "retaliation for each and every Jew murdered by the White Paper". He stressed that solidarity and commonality of purpose within the Yishuv, and especially among the underground factions, were imperative for the struggle against the British Mandate to succeed.

Taking Ben-Gurion's letter as the Jewish Agency's endorsement of fresh military actions against the British in Palestine, Sneh called off the persecution of Irgun fighters and initiated a merging of the Haganah, the Irgun and Lehi under a single authority, the United Resistance.

The leadership comprised two Haganah representatives—Yisrael Galili and Moshe Sneh; one from the Irgun—Menachem Begin; and one from Lehi—Nathan Yellin-Mor. All operations would require authorization from the Haganah command after discussions with Palmach, the Irgun and Lehi chiefs of operations: Yitzhak Sadeh, Eitan Livni and Yaakov Eliav respectively. Dubbed the 'Night of the Trains', on 1 November the United Resistance revealed its intentions against the British mandatory power through widespread guerrilla-style actions. The Haganah's military resistance against the British would last nine months, from November 1945 to July 1946.

During the night, Haganah operatives detonated 500 explosive devices on the rail network, causing major regional rail traffic disruptions, while the Palmach sank two police patrol boats in Haifa. At Lydda, Livni led Irgun fighters in a major attack on the railway station, inflicting serious damage and casualties. At Haifa, Lehi members attacked the oil refinery. The coordinated attacks resulted in the deaths of a British soldier, a Palestine policeman and two Palestine rail workers.

Britain was outraged, but for once the Jewish Agency was noticeably circumspect in its anticipated reaction. Whilst confirming the agency's abhorrence of violence to achieve a political solution, it "realizes that its ability to impose restraint has been severely tested by the continued policy [of the British government], which the Jews regard as fatal for them".

On the night of 27 December, combined Irgun–Lehi strike units carried out attacks on the British CID HQ in Jerusalem, the CID branch in Jaffa and the army

---

* Begin.

Damage to the Allenby Bridge carrying the main road from Palestine to Transjordan following an attack by underground saboteurs, June 1946. (Photo Sergeant Gregory)

camp at the Tel Aviv Exhibition Grounds. Despite increased British security at the Russian Compound on Jerusalem's Jaffa Road, at 7.15 p.m. a joint underground force, commanded by Polish-born Irgun fighter Shraga Alis, gained access to the main building to lay explosive charges. As the devices detonated, the building collapsed. In a report carried in the Hull *Daily Mail* of 28 December, it was said that there had been a series of explosions, in which a British policeman (Constable G. F. Smith) and four Basuto soldiers on guard duty were killed. Several British policemen, having survived the explosions, set off down Jaffa Road in the direction of the Orion Cinema in pursuit of the fleeing Jewish assailants. In a series of running exchanges of gunfire, constables Nicholson and Hyde were shot and killed. Toward the cinema, Assistant Superintendent F. Flanagan met the same fate.

In Jaffa, under cover of darkness, senior Irgun commander Eliyahu Tamler led a raid on the four-storey CID building on the Jaffa–Tel Aviv road. The bomb they planted destroyed the second floor of the building that housed the British intelligence offices.

In Tel Aviv the talented Irgun commander, Amichai 'Gidi' Paglin, who would go on to organize the King David Hotel bombing and the Acre prison breakout, led a force in an unsuccessful raid on the Corps of Royal Electrical and Mechanical Engineers (REME) workshops in Tel Aviv, where it was believed that a consignment of weapons had been stored. Lance-Corporal Sharp of the British Army and Irgun fighter Dov Sternglass lost their lives during the raid.

Arguably, one of the most daring and successful combined operations under the United Resistance umbrella took place when raids were simultaneously launched against three RAF airfields on the night of 25/26 February 1946.

Built as RAF Petah Tikva (Petach Tiqwa) in 1941, the Kfar Sirkin airfield was located seven miles east of Tel Aviv. At 8.40 p.m., Lehi fighters breached the perimeter security fence, sprinting toward parked Spitfire aircraft in the dispersal area while other

Old Bren carrier at Petah Tikva. (Photo Israel Free Image)

elements of the force provided covering fire. With armoured vehicles of the RAF Regiment pinned down under heavy fire, the attackers planted explosives in the radiators and cockpits of Supermarine Spitfire LF9s of No. 32 and No.208 squadrons, destroying seven in the ensuing blasts.

At Lydda airfield (now Ben-Gurion International Airport), four miles from Kfar Sirkin, Irgun commander Dov 'Shimshon' Cohen was running behind schedule. In the centre of the field, two tents marked the post from where RAF Bren carriers patrolled the perimeter, with the white glare of a searchlight situated on the control tower beaming across the expanse. Across the road from the airfield, stood the RAF Regiment garrison. The odds were heavily stacked against his team of saboteurs, but even as he could discern the distant thudding of explosives going off at Kfar Sirkin, Cohen proceeded with the attack. When explosives set on an electrical transformer by some of his men went off and sudden darkness flooded the airfield, fighters breached the security fence and dashed towards the dispersed aircraft. On the outside of the fence, other members of the unit enfiladed the RAF barracks to keep the troops away from the airfield. Explosions destroyed two Avro Anson multirole and two light communication aircraft.

At the same time, two truckloads of Irgun fighters with weapons and explosives approached RAF Qastina airfield (now Hatzor Israeli Air Force Base) from Rehovot. Working silently under the command of Paglin, the wire of the perimeter fence was cut, allowing a group of Irgun sappers with ladders to slip through and head off in the direction of the dark shapes of Handley Page Halifax VII transports of No. 644 Squadron parked in the dispersal area. Explosive charges were placed where the wings joined the fuselage, and time fuses attached.

As a sequence of deafening explosions rent the still night, Irgun machine-gunners directed heavy fire into the RAF barracks. Six of the Halifax aircraft were destroyed and a further five subsequently written off as beyond economic repair. As the Irgun fighters fled the carnage, one of their number, Nazim Ezra Ajami, was shot and killed, becoming the only underground fatality of the night's three raids.

In an audacious daylight raid on 6 March, a truckload of Irgun fighters, dressed as British soldiers, drove up to the main gate of the sprawling British Army Sarafand al Amar cantonment three miles northwest of Ramla. Overcoming the gate guards with relative ease, they brazenly drove down to the camp armoury where they loaded the truck with as many packing cases of weapons and boxes of ammunition as the truck could take. Before leaving, Irgun operation commander Eliyahu Tamler set off a landmine in the armoury to destroy remaining arms and ammunition.

By this time, the alarm had been raised. An increasing number of British troops descended on the armoury where, in a firefight, five Irgun fighters were wounded, Yosef Simchon and Michael Ashbel seriously so. While being rushed to hospital in

Members of the King's Shropshire Light Infantry in Palestine. (Photo Sergeant Gregory)

Tel Aviv, the two men were apprehended at a British Army roadblock. Simchon and Ashbel survived to appear before a military tribunal, at which they were convicted of terrorism and sentenced to death.

On 18 June, the Irgun proved to the British authorities that they would enforce the Law of Moses: "Just as another person has received injury from him, so it will be given to him." (Lev. 24:19). Irgun units raided the Gat Rimon and Hayarkon hotels in Tel Aviv, where British officers were quartered, and abducted six officers—five army and one RAF—as a ransom to stop their two comrades from being taken to the gallows. Special correspondent for *The Press and Journal* in Jerusalem, J. L. Hays, reporting in the *Aberdeen Press and Journal* of 19 June, stated, "The kidnapping seems likely to be the work of the smaller 'Irgun Zvai Leumi', the national military organisation with 40,000 members which was originally associated with the neo-fascist Revisionist Party." The Jewish Agency described the abduction as "an act of lunacy".

After thirty-six hours' captivity in a house in Jerusalem's Bucharim quarter, Major H. P Chadwick of the East Yorkshire Regiment escaped from his captors. However, captains G. C. Warburton, D. T. Rae, A. E. Taylor and K. H. Spencer, and Flight Lieutenant P. A. E. Russell would only return to freedom when the British High Commissioner commuted the Simchon and Ashbel death sentences to life imprisonment.

During the night of 2/3 April, seventy-five Irgun fighters, split into three groups and spread over an area of twenty-six miles, conducted a major operation against the Palestine rail network. Bridges, culverts, telephone poles and miles of track were destroyed, causing critical disruption. The northern force under Menahem Schiff (Zeev), upon successfully completing their task, was able to withdraw safely while under fire from a British unit. However, the two other groups would pay the price.

The eastern force came under fire while placing explosive charges, during which Ezra Rabia was severely wounded. As the attackers withdrew across the dunes toward Bat Yam sixteen miles away, Rabia died of his wounds. For Dov Cohen's southern force, the withdrawal, after successfully destroying several railway installations and a locomotive, was more traumatic. Withdrawal across the dunes was tedious and therefore progress slow. At first light, with Bat Yam in sight, an RAF reconnaissance plane spotted the exhausted fighters. In a short space of time Cohen and his men were enveloped by British paratroops, and in the ensuing firefight, Avner Ben-Shem was killed and four other Irgun fighters wounded. Thirty-one fighters were captured, including Eitan Livni, the Irgun's chief operations officer. All were sentenced to fifteen years imprisonment. Cohen was able to avoid capture.

Over the following weeks, sporadic attacks and raids were carried out by both combined underground forces, as well as by the three individual movements within the United Resistance. This loose arrangement in which the Haganah, the Irgun and Lehi appeared to enjoy considerable autonomy—contrary to the spirit of the tripartite

Soldiers of the 6th Airborne Division removing a German MG 34 machine gun from a hidden cache of weapons found in the Jewish settlement of Doroth near Gaza. (Photo Sergeant Turner)

agreement—served to divide and confuse the Yishuv. The sought-after, and necessary, need to coordinate military action against the mandatory power was facing diminishing effectiveness. As the largest nationalist force, the Haganah continually strived to ensure that targeted objectives excluded the taking of life where possible. Understandably, when armed clashes occurred, the rules of combat and survival pertained.

One such 'independent', ill-conceived action by members of Lehi on 25 April would have major repercussions on the Irgun, the Haganah and the long-suffering Yishuv in general. It would also further harden the British administration's governance of Palestine.

At 8.45 p.m., an estimated forty armed men and women launched an attack on the British 6th Airborne Division carpark opposite the Apak Quarter police station on the Tel Aviv–Jaffa boundary. The guard tent, from which ten soldiers of the 5th (Scottish) Parachute Battalion, Lydda Brigade, performed their guard duties, was bombed and any soldier that moved was fired at. In the first direct attack on the British military by Jewish activists, seven members of the 6th Airborne Division were killed, two as they slept.

The division's commander, Major-General James Cassels, in a terse missive brimming with vitriol, reacted to Tel Aviv Acting Mayor Perelson's expression of regret:

I have received your message of regret but I have sent for you today to say how horrified and disgusted I am at the outrage committed by the Jews on the night of April 25, when seven British soldiers were wilfully and brutally murdered by members of your community.

As a result I have decided to impose certain restrictions on the Jewish community as a whole. My decision to restrict the whole community has been made in order to maintain public scrutiny and because I hold the community to blame.

There is no doubt in my mind that many members either knew of this project or could have given some warning before it happened.

However, Cassel's understandable but unprofessional outburst against anyone who was a Jew in Palestine produced strong and bitter resentment among both the British military and the Yishuv. The Anglo-American special committee's report on the Palestinian issue only served to highlight growing polarization beyond the mandate's borders. US President Harry S. Truman wanted London to allow 100,000 misplaced European Jews into Palestine, while Bevin advocated a bi-national state comprising a Jewish and an Arab province. Prime Minister Atlee, on the other hand, refused to consider Jewish immigration until all underground terror movements, with the full collaboration of the Jewish Agency, were disbanded. The Arab League called on Truman to refrain from interfering, while insisting the British immediately commence Anglo-Arab negotiations for the creation of an independent Arab state in Palestine.

After careful, in-depth planning, in the early hours of 29 June the British authorities hit back. In what was more commonly referred to as 'Black Sabbath' or 'Black Saturday', Operation Agatha saw a countrywide curfew imposed as 17,000 British troops descended on identified Jewish targets. Some 2,700 Jews were arrested and interned at a special camp at Rafiah. The Jewish Agency

A Jewish underground fighter stashing rifles. (Israel GPO)

buildings in Jerusalem were raided and large quantities of current and archival documents seized. Taken to the seat of the government secretariat and military command in the King David Hotel, the material revealed an irrefutable link between the Jewish Agency and the command of the United Resistance. The text of the tripartite underground alliance was discovered, in addition to signals granting the Irgun and Lehi the authority to hit British targets. Members of the Jewish Agency executive were arrested at their homes and transported to the special 'VIP camp' at Latrun.

Kibbutzim were also raided to conduct routine searches. At Kibbutz Yagur, British troops uncovered a substantial arms cache, which included 300 rifles, 100 2-inch mortars, 400,000 rounds of ammunition, 5,000 grenades and 78 sidearms. Within days of Operation Agatha, the Haganah felt the need to retaliate to show the authorities that the underground resistance remained a strong force.

On 1 July, head of the Haganah command Moshe Sneh wrote to Begin:

a) At the earliest possible opportunity, you are to carry out the operation at the 'chick' [King David Hotel] and at the house of "your servant and messiah" [David Brothers building]. Inform me of the date. Preferably at the same time. Do not reveal the identity of the implementing body—either by announcing it explicitly or by hinting.
b) We too are preparing something [raid on the Bat Galim army camp]—will inform you of details in good time.
c) Exclude TA [Tel Aviv] from any plan of action. We are all interested in preserving TA—as the center of Yishuv life and the centre of our own activities. If, as the result of any action, TA is immobilized (curfew, arrests), this will paralyse us and our plans as well. And the important objects of the other side are not focused here. Hence, TA is 'out of bounds' for the forces of Israel.*

The Irgun had been nominated to destroy the mandatory power's nerve centre by blowing up the King David Hotel in Jerusalem, codenamed Operation Chick. The Lehi-planned attack on the David Brothers building was cancelled.

At this critical time, an ailing president of the World Zionist Organization, Chaim Weizmann, sent a message with an emissary to Sneh. Exercising his right as commander of the armed forces, Weizmann demanded that "you cease all this activity". Sneh put the order to the X Committee, the supreme political committee that authorized or rejected operational plans of the United Resistance, which, by majority vote, acquiesced. Sneh, however, was not in favour of terminating the activities of the underground resistance and resigned his post in protest. Retaining his role as liaison officer

---

* Jabotinsky Institute Archives, k-4 1/11/5.

Smite the Enemy Hard

The imposing edifice of the King David Hotel, 1938. (Photo Israel GPO)

with the Irgun and Lehi, Sneh met with Begin to inform him of a postponement in the intended bombing of the King David Hotel, but withheld the X Committee's decision. The date of the attack was pushed back to Monday, 22 July 1946.

Opened in 1931, the construction of the six-storey King David Hotel had been financed by wealthy Egyptian Jews. Situated on King David Street in the centre of Jerusalem, with views over the Old City and Mount Zion, the southern wing was converted into British administrative and military headquarters during the mandate. A neighbouring building housed the British military police and the Special Investigations Branch. By 1946, the hotel resembled a fortress, complete with a reinforced barbed-wire perimeter barricade and machine-gun posts. A network of alarms would warn hundreds of security personnel in the building in the event of a terrorist attack.

The plan for the attack was masterminded by Irgun commander Amihai 'Gidi' Paglin, a veteran of the underground struggle. For weeks Irgun operatives maintained a fulltime reconnaissance of the hotel. From the findings, Paglin identified a significant weakness in the British ring of steel: the hotel kitchen. A constant stream of delivery vehicles would arrive at the kitchen's outside door during the day, the receiving area a short distance from a basement under the secretariat. Here, pillars supported the six floors above.

At 7 a.m. on that Monday, individual Irgun fighters began assembling at the Bet Aharon Talmud Torah seminary in Jerusalem. They guessed that an operation was in the offing, but that is all they knew. Following a briefing from the very young operation commander, Yisrael 'Gidon' Levi, weapons were issued and roles allocated.

Disguised as Arabs and led by Yosef Avni, a forward group of fighters left for the hotel by bus. There, at a side entrance, these 'porters' would wait to assist with the unloading of the explosives. The strike force was the next to leave the seminary, their van loaded with seven milk churns, each packed with 50kg of TNT-gelignite explosives, primed with detonators and time fuses. Levi was dressed as a Sudanese waiter, while the rest of the team in the van were dressed as Arabs.

At around noon, the arrival of the strike force was preceded by two small diversionary explosions, one in the hotel grounds to the south, and the other in the lane leading to the French Consulate. Arriving at the hotel's side entrance, the guards were easily overcome. Once inside, hotel staff rounded up in the immediate vicinity were herded into the kitchen. With the aid of the 'porters', the milk churns were lugged in and placed next to the supporting pillars. Levi set the timer for thirty minutes and ordered his men out. Eight minutes after their arrival, the strike force sped off in their van, but by this time the alarm had been raised and a firefight ensued. Two Irgun fighters were wounded, including Aharon Abramovitch who succumbed to his wounds a while later.

When he had left the hotel building, Levi ordered two female Irgun fighters to execute their specific mission in the operation. Dashing to a nearby telephone booth, the two women left a chilling message with the hotel reception desk and the *Palestine Post* editorial office:

> I am speaking on behalf of the Hebrew underground.
> We have placed an explosive device in the hotel.
> Evacuate it at once—you have been warned.*

However, the Irgun's warnings, issued in an apparent attempt to keep casualties to a minimum, went unheeded. At 12.37 p.m. the milk churns exploded, collapsing the hotel's whole south wing. The Irgun claimed sole responsibility, and after ten days of rubble clearing by elements of the British Corps of Engineers and members of the 6th Airborne Division, the death toll amounted to ninety-one: twenty-eight Britons, forty-one Arabs, seventeen Jews and five other nationalities. Forty-six were injured, including Assistant Secretary Downing Thompson who died of his injuries a week later.

The shocked leaders of the Jewish Agency condemned the operation, while Ben-Gurion denounced the Irgun as "the enemy of the Jewish people". The Jewish press and Haganah publications joined the chorus of outrage.

---

* www.etzel.org.il

Above left: British troops search for survivors in the collapsed wing of the King David Hotel. (Photo Israel GPO)

Above right: British policemen and troops tend to an injured survivor of the bombing of the King David Hotel. (Photo Israel GPO)

On 5 August, at a meeting of the Jewish Agency Executive in Paris, it was resolved to end armed resistance against the British in Palestine, effectively dissolving the United Resistance. The Haganah now focused on bringing illegal immigrants into Palestine, and preventing British shipping from deporting others.

The Irgun—and Lehi—vowed to continue their struggle against the British Mandate. After ten months in the United Resistance, the Irgun had grown stronger. Numbers had increased and stocks of weapons and ammunition pilfered from British sources had grown. No longer having to operate under the authority of the Haganah command, the Irgun intensified its fight against the British Mandate.

5. AN EYE FOR AN EYE

> Ever since the British murderers "sentenced" the Hebrew prisoners of war, Ashbel and Simchon, to death—we warned repeatedly that if the enemy dared to violate the rules of law and hanged our captured comrades—we would set up gallows for their captors.
>
> The murderous enemy, thirsting for blood, did not heed our warnings. He led nine Hebrew prisoners to the gallows. Consequently we hanged his spies. Not as a "reprisal"—for there is no adequate reprisal for the unclean oppressor.
>
> Irgun statement, July 1947[*]

The months of August and September 1946 were quiet in the aftermath of the King David Hotel bombing. The Irgun started looking at Europe in which to extend its recruiting and procurement of war matériel activities, and to facilitate Jewish immigration into Palestine. The Irgun representatives in charge of 'diaspora operations' had been in place since the previous year: Ely 'Pesach' Tavin in Rome and Dr Shmuel 'Elhanan' Ariel in Paris.

In Italy, Tavin had established cells under an umbrella organization of "partisans and ghetto fighters", called Balahav. A newspaper, the *Irgunpress*, was circulated in English, German, French and Italian, while propaganda leaflets were distributed in refugee camps and among local Italians. In October, new Irgun high command appointee, Samuel Katz, travelled from Palestine to Paris where he met with Tavin and Ariel. The former was handed orders from the high command to commence anti-British operations in Italy. However, in France a private agreement was reached in which the Irgun would not conduct operations in that country in return for transit permits from the Interior Ministry for 30,000 Jewish refugees.

In the evening of 31 October, two teams of Irgun fighters set off on their missions in Rome. One painted a large swastika on a wall of the British Consulate, while the other planted two explosive devices in the British Embassy. The resultant explosions caused major damage to two floors of the embassy. The Irgun issued a statement through an American journalist, claiming responsibility and warning that London would be next. The British government reacted immediately, stepping up security at airports, harbours and key instillations. In some circles, it was firmly believed that the Irgun had already established an underground network in the capital. This was not the case, but for the Irgun it was a silent victory.

---

[*] Tavin & Alexander.

A Vickers machine-gun team of the 2nd Battalion, Middlesex Regiment, in Palestine. (Photo Sergeant Gregory)

In Palestine, an Irgun operation to blow up the Jerusalem train station saw the fighters walk into a British Army ambush at the station building. Upon being discovered, the men fled to the two taxis waiting for them outside, leaving behind primed suitcases of explosives. As they left the building, they were fired on from every direction. Feinstein, Azulai, Horovitz and Biton all sustained gunshot wounds, and were later arrested by the British police. Meir Feinstein appeared before a military tribunal where he was convicted and sentenced to death. Half an hour before his execution on 21 April 1947, together with Moshe Barazani, he took his own life.

It transpired that senior Irgun commander Heinrich 'Yanai' Reinhold, second-in-command during the attack on the King David Hotel, had betrayed his comrades. Reinhold had been arrested and interrogated over the hotel attack, during which he made the decision to collaborate with the British police to save his own neck from the hangman's noose.

Through November, the number of Irgun acts of sabotage escalated, with a marked increase in the use of electrically detonated mines. British casualty rates rose accordingly. On 9 November, an Irgun bomb killed four British policemen in the Bukharan Quarter of Jerusalem. *The Scotsman* reported: "The body of one policeman was found three streets away; another was discovered on a roof 200 yards distant." Three British policemen and an RAF sergeant were killed and six policemen injured when, on 17 November, Irgun fighters detonated a mine under a police patrol truck in Lydda. The following day, in ill-disciplined retaliation, British troops drove down Tel Aviv's Hayarkon Street, discharging weapons and smashing shops and cafés.

With unchecked emotions entering the quagmire that was the Palestine 'problem', the mandatory courts waded in with what most described as archaic punishment that should have remained in the era of slavery and on the decks of nineteenth-century Royal Navy war ships. Having been found guilty of carrying arms during the robbery of a Jaffa bank, in December Irgun fighter Benjamin Kimchi was sentenced by a British Mandate court to eighteen years' imprisonment *and* eighteen lashes. Abject disbelief swept through the Yishuv and the diaspora. In *The Revolt*, Menachem Begin summed up the incredulity of the rationale behind the flogging part of the sentence:

> Certain elements in the machinery of British government seem to have a special affection for the use of the whip.
>
> In the development of certain British Colonies the whip had been made to serve an educational purpose. It is applied, of course, not to recalcitrant boys but to adults who are treated like disorderly children. When I travelled through Persia on my way from Russia to Eretz Israel, I saw this symbol of British rule. Although Persia was not, at any rate formally, a British Colony, every British officer carried a cane or a little whip and regularly emphasized his orders to the "natives" with a light and pedagogic touch of one of these "spectres of gentle peace."
>
> While Eretz Israel was ruled as a British Colony, it could not logically be denied the educational privilege of the whip.*

The day after the ill-conceived sentencing, the RPF machinery plastered walls throughout the mandate with a poster in English and Hebrew:

> WARNING!
>
> A Hebrew soldier, taken prisoner by the enemy, was sentenced by an illegal British "court" to the humiliating punishment of flogging.
>
> We warn the occupation Government not to carry out this punishment, which is contrary to the laws of soldiers' honour. If it is put into effect—every officer of the British occupation in Eretz Israel will be liable to be punished in the same way: *to get 18 whips.*†

---

* Begin.
† J. Bowyer Bell, *Terror Out of Zion* (St James Press, London, 1977).

An Eye for an Eye

A British Army patrol moves down Nahlat Benyamin Street in Tel Aviv, 1947. (Photo Israel GPO)

General Sir Evelyn Barker, General Officer Commanding of the British Forces in Palestine and Trans-Jordan from 1946 to 1947, and known for his anti-Semitic views, ignored the warning.

On the 27th—the Sabbath—the sixteen-year-old Kimchi was taken from his cell, and in private given eighteen lashes. Abhorrence of Britain and her instruments of power boiled over, the Irgun declaring, albeit rather theatrically: "Let the sound of these lashes echo; let it reverberate; Hark you who have survived the foul purposes of Hitler who in the light of contemporary events is slowly taking on the shape of a gentleman!"

On the evening of Sunday the 29th, armed elements of the Hok, the Irgun's combat division, brazenly strode into the lobby of the Hotel Metropole in the coastal diamond city of Netanya where they grabbed the unsuspecting Major 'Paddy' Brett DSO, MC, of the 2nd Parachute Brigade and bundled him into a waiting car. Driven to a grove of eucalyptus trees, Brett was stripped to his underwear, his 'sentence' was read out, and he was dealt eighteen lashes. He was driven back to the hotel, but his trousers were not returned. In Rishon LeZion, five miles south of Tel Aviv, Sergeant Terence Gillam was abducted from Café Theresa and taken fifty yards down the street where he was given eighteen lashes. In Tel Aviv itself, two British Army sergeants were forcibly removed from the Armon Hotel by ten members of the Hok and driven to Hadassah Park near the zoological gardens where they were bound to trees and each given eighteen lashes.

A British Army roadblock checking vehicles on the Jerusalem Highway, 1947. (Photo Israel GPO)

Fresh RPF posters went up promising: "If the oppressors dare in the future to abuse the bodies and the human and national honour of Jewish youths, we shall no longer reply with the whip. *We shall reply with fire.*"*

There would be no further floggings of Jewish prisoners in the mandate.

That night, the British military responded immediately. Armoured cars equipped with loudspeakers drove down Tel Aviv's streets, ordering all 6th Airborne Division troops to return to barracks. A dusk-to-dawn curfew was imposed, followed by large cordon-and-search operations in Tel Aviv, Netanya and Rishon LeZion in an intensive hunt for those responsible for the armed abduction and flogging of the four British soldiers.

At one such roadblock on the Lydda airport road in the city of Kfar Saba—an Irgun operational area—a car carrying five Irgun fighters from Petah Tikva on a similar mission, was stopped in a brief shootout with British troops. The driver, Avraham Mizrahi was shot and killed. The leader, twenty-four-year-old Polish-born Yehiel Drezner—using the name Dov Rosenbaum—was arrested, together with Mordechai Alkahi (22), Eliezer Kashani (24) and Haim 'Gilad' Golovsky (17).

On 10 February 1947, the four appeared before a military court on capital charges. Refusing to recognize the legitimacy of the court, the men refused to have anything

---

* Ibid.

to do with the proceedings, other than to make well-prepared defiant statements against the British Mandate. After only ninety minutes, the court returned a verdict of guilty. Due to his age, Golovsky was sentenced to life imprisonment, while the other three were sentenced to death by hanging. At Jerusalem Central Prison they joined fellow Irgun fighter, Dov Gruner, to await their destiny.

Throughout January 1947, the Irgun continued to hit British military and police targets. On the 15th, it was announced that there would be a phased deployment of the British 3rd (Iron) Infantry Division into the mandate, forming part of the Middle East Land Forces. Severe restrictions were placed on the movement of British military and law-enforcement personnel: cinemas, cafés and large public areas were declared out of bounds and troops were ordered to walk in groups of not less than four. Operation Polly was launched. All dependents were withdrawn into security zones prior to being removed from the mandate. Throughout the territory there was clear evidence of a tightening of security: sandbags, barbed wire, checkpoints, machine-gun posts, barricades, troops and police. The mandate resembled a besieged war zone.

Tel Aviv under siege. Elements of the 6th Airborne Division guard a key building.

On 24 January—a Sabbath—Barker confirmed the death sentence on Gruner:

> I am in favour of the death penalty for murder, political or otherwise. The one strict law we had was against carrying arms. And it's no good having a law like that if you don't enforce it. So if anyone was caught carrying arms, he was up before a court martial, he could state his case, but if he was found guilty that was it. And, subject to Alan Cunningham's [the High Commissioner of Palestine] final say, I would confirm the death sentence.*

That Sunday, members of Irgun took retired British Army major H. A. I. Collins and Tel Aviv judge Ralph Windham hostage, precipitating Gruner's stay of execution. The two hostages were released.

The Irgun continued to apply pressure on the British establishment. Following Barker's confirmation in February of the death sentence on Drezner, Alkahi and Kashani, on 1 March the Irgun launched an attack—one of sixteen operations on the day—on the Jerusalem British officers' club in Goldschmidt House. As a Bren gun sited on King George Avenue, opposite the Yeshurun Synagogue, opened fire on the building, a five-man combat unit, led by Dov 'Yishai' Salomon, crashed their van through the barbed-wire security perimeter. Lugging rucksacks holding 90 kilograms of explosive into the building, the fighters found the building's support pillars against which the explosives were placed and the fuses ignited. At 3.30 p.m. the explosives detonated, demolishing the side of the building. In an official communiqué released on the Monday, the death toll was put at thirteen: two British Army officers, a British soldier, a police officer and nine NAAFI civilians. Ten members of the security forces and six NAAFI civilians were injured.

British High Commissioner (General rtd.) Sir Alan Cunningham immediately activated operations Elephant and Hippo. Martial law was introduced in the Jewish quarters of northern Jerusalem (Hippo) and in the districts of Tel Aviv (Elephant), Ramat Gan, Bnei Barak and Petah Tikva, and 20,000 troops deployed to conduct intensive cordon-and-search operations.

The whole anti-terrorist operation was, however, a dismal and embarrassing failure for the mandatory forces. As few as seventy-eight suspected terrorists were apprehended, with only twelve positively identified as members of the Irgun. The costly exercise did nothing to stall, let alone stop, the underground's reign of terror, and on 17 March, martial law was lifted.

In Britain the press bayed "govern or get out", increasing public pressure for an end to the Palestine Mandate débâcle, and on 2 April, London once more resorted to the

---

* Nicholas Bethell, *The Palestine Triangle: The Struggle for the Holy Land, 1935–48* (Putnam, New York, 1979).

United Nations in an attempt to find a political solution to what had clearly become an ungovernable mandate. At Lake Success in New York, temporary home of the UN, the Soviet Union endorsed Britain's request to have the Palestine question placed on the agenda of the General Assembly and for the convening of a special session to consider the issue. On 28 April, the First Special Session commenced its task. At a meeting of the Jewish National Council in Palestine at the beginning of the month, Ben-Gurion called for the Jewish people to crush terrorism: "If need be we shall speak to them in the only language they understand—force."*

In the far northern Mediterranean coastal plain of the mandate, sits the ancient city of Acre. In the old city, a citadel had been constructed during the Ottoman period over the ruins of a twelfth-century Crusader fortress. At the time of the British Mandate, the fortress served as a high-security prison. Surrounded by a deep moat to the east and north and the Mediterranean to the west, the building was in the centre of an Arab town void of any Jewish inhabitants. It was to the prison's death row that Gruner, Drezner, Alkahi and Kashani were transferred from Jerusalem on 14 April.

At 4 a.m. on the morning of Wednesday, 16 April, while singing the Zionist anthem, *Hatikvah*, the four men were taken to the courtyard gallows and hanged. Confined to their homes in the prelude to the executions, 600,000 Jews heard the radio broadcast about the hangings and an extension of the curfew.

The Irgun had declared:

> On the very day of his leaving, the murderer [Barker] in General's uniform left a "souvenir" to the country: an order to kill three Hebrew war-prisoners. The haste was unusual; the procedure was set aside—hurry, hurry, Barker must use his last chance to murder three sons of the hated race.
>
> Surely they are all glad now. Barker is glad that he "succeeded" in avenging his bitter defeats. The so-called "socialist" Government is also glad; Churchill will be given proof that it is composed of "men".
>
> The question however is to be asked how long they will be glad? We do not find it necessary to reiterate our warning in connection with the murder of prisoners. Killing defenceless prisoners of war is one of the basest crimes.
>
> If the crime is committed, the Underground will do its duty. It will do it under any circumstances. And the responsibility for all that will occur in this country after the cold-blooded murder of our comrades will rest with the murderers.
>
> Irgun statement, 'Fighting Judea No. 6'†

---

* *Aberdeen Press and Journal*, 2 April 1947.
† Tavin & Alexander.

Irgun: Revisionist Zionism 1931–1948

Clockwise from above left: Dov Gruner, Yehiel Drezner, Mordechai Alkahi and Eliezer Kashani. (Photos Israel GPO)

An Eye for an Eye

A car bomb explodes in a Jerusalem street, 1948.

Promises of eye-for-an-eye revenge notwithstanding, the Revisionists had effectively acquired a further four *Olei Hagardom* (those hanged in the gallows) martyrs for the liberation struggle. A week later, the names of Irgun member Meir Feinstein and Lehi member Moshe Barazani would be added to the roll when they used a smuggled-in grenade to take their lives shortly before their scheduled executions.

For the rest of the month, Irgun operatives failed to abduct suitable British mandatory personnel for retributive hangings. Several military vehicles were ambushed on 21 April, and on the 23rd, a landmine was detonated under a troop train on the Cairo–Haifa line near Rehovot, derailing the train and killing eight—including five British soldiers—and injuring forty-one. Three days later, a Postal Signals Service van hijacked by Irgun fighters and loaded with explosives, was driven in broad daylight into the heavily defended Serona police camp, the largest in Palestine. A British police officer, Inspector Allen Trutwein, and constables Stanley Barnes, Alan Casey and Ronald Davies were killed when the bomb exploded.

On the eve of the convening of the UN's Special Committee on Palestine (UNSCOP), the Irgun issued a press statement declaring:

> There will be no peace in Palestine, the Middle East or the world, until the British occupation regime in Palestine and Trans-Jordan is abolished and the

British forces withdrawn ... Britain is going to the United Nations only for new international approval of her rule in Palestine.*

All the while, at the Irgun HQ the indomitable chief operations officer, Amichai 'Gidi' Paglin, worked untiringly on a plan to spring Irgun and Lehi prisoners from the Acre Prison. Of the eighty-two underground fighters incarcerated in the thick-walled fortress, it was agreed that only forty-one could be freed and comfortably hidden in the Yishuv. Eitan Livni, the most senior Irgun prisoner, who had pinpointed a breakout point in the south wall, would select the escapees.

Dov 'Shimshon' Cohen would command the twenty-three-man combat unit, the majority dressed in British Corps of Engineers uniforms and a few in Arab attire. On Sunday, 4 May, dressed as a British Army captain, Cohen set off in the command jeep at the head of a convoy of five military and two civilian vehicles. Upon arrival at Acre, two of the vehicles drove into the adjacent market where they started 'repair work' on telephone lines. Led by Dov Salomon, the fighters used ladders to scale the roof of the Turkish bath to gain access to the prison wall. Explosive charges were hoisted up and attached to prison windows.

Meanwhile, outside, other members of the team scattered mines along the roads leading to the breakout site. Another three-man team had set up a mortar to the north of the city, ready to fire into the nearby army camp at the appointed time. At a service station situated at the entrance to the new city, the command jeep pulled up to lay landmines and to torch the garage.

At 3 p.m. the cell doors were opened for the routine afternoon exercise, and at 4.22 p.m. a massive explosion rent the air, blasting a large hole in the fortress wall. In the chaos and shooting, compounded by scores of Arabs exploiting their unexpected chance at freedom, the forty-one selected Irgun and Lehi prisoners escaped through the gap in the wall. The first group of thirteen escapees clambered into a van which immediately sped off, but in the confusion, the driver headed for Haifa instead of Mount Napoleon. By the time he had realized his error and tried to turn around, a group of British soldiers who had been relaxing on the beach opened fire on the van, causing it to crash and overturn.

Climbing out of the wrecked van, Cohen and the escapees sprinted in the direction of the service station, closely pursued by the soldiers. But for Cohen, firing his Bren gun to cover his comrades, it was the end of his fight against the British, as he was cut down by seventeen bullets fired from British firearms. Another member of his team, Zalman Lifshitz, was also killed. When the firing stopped it revealed five dead escapees and six wounded. Only two of the prisoners were untouched and were returned to the prison.

---

* *Aberdeen Press and Journal*, 28 April 1947.

An Eye for an Eye

Acre Prison. (Photo Dutch National Archives)

Fighters manning two Irgun blocking units failed to hear the bugle signalling them to withdraw, and after a prolonged firefight with British troops, Avshalom Haviv, Meir Nakar, Yaakov Weiss, Amnon Michaeli and Menahem Ostrowicz were captured. The other escapees succeeded in getting away safely.

The post mortem revealed that twenty Irgun and seven Lehi prisoners had been sprung, but at the cost of six escapees and three fighters killed in clashes with British security forces. Official sources stated that 131 Arabs also escaped.

Three weeks later, Avshalom Haviv, Meir Nakar and Yaakov Weiss were found guilty of carrying weapons and sentenced to death.

While anti-mandate rhetoric spread in the House of Commons in the wake of yet another crisis in Palestine, in New York the Soviet permanent representative to the UN, Andrei Gromyko, stunned London, Washington and the Arab League, when he used the platform of the international body on 14 May to challenge the

UNSCOP by insisting that they "must take certain obvious facts into account—firstly the Arab revolts and secondly the bloody incidents at present occurring there". Attacking Britain for what he referred to as the "bankruptcy of the mandatory system in Palestine", the hard-line professional diplomat with the apt moniker 'Grim Grom', stressed:

1. The United Nations cannot tolerate the continued suffering of Jews in Europe today, after 6,000,000 were killed by the Nazis.
2. The United Nations has a duty towards the Jewish survivors of Nazi brutality.
3. The study of a possible Jewish State should one of the most important tasks of the Fact-finding Commission.*

Had the global Jewish community found a new champion from a wholly unexpected and unlikely quarter? Any Soviet pressure on UNSCOP to heed Gromyko's 'guidance' might have been the subject of conjecture, but the eleven-nation committee had agreed to meet with the Irgun during a fact-finding mission to Palestine. Ironically, the delegation arrived on 16 June, the day that the president of the military court in Jerusalem imposed the death sentence on three of the Irgun prisoners: Avshalom Haviv, Meir Nakar and Yaakov Weiss.

To set the tone for the meeting with UNSCOP, scheduled for 24 June, the Irgun high command sent an official letter to the committee, the subject matter almost entirely dedicated to the three Irgun fighters on death row, in a bid to win a stay of execution:

> In a memorandum which we shall present to the Committee during the next few days we shall inter alia deal with the crimes the British Government have committed against our people ...
>
> The witnesses who are able to submit to the Committee the most important facts relating to this charge against the British administration are: Yaacov Weiss, Meir Nakar, and Avshalom Haviv, who themselves witnessed and personally experienced the criminal behaviour of the British security forces to prisoners and wounded.
>
> These three prisoners are at present in the condemned cell at the Acre Gaol. They were 'sentenced' to death by a British military 'court' and they stand in imminent danger of being murdered. The Occupation authorities may desire to hasten their execution in order to prevent their appearing before the Committee. The question of their being called to testify, therefore, brooks no delay.

---

* *Nottingham Journal*, 15 May 1947.

An Eye for an Eye

Clockwise from above left: Avshalom Haviv, Meir Nakar and Yaakov Weiss. (Photos Israel GPO)

> We respectfully propose to the Committee that it demand of the British Occupation Government the removal of the threat of murder of the three prisoners, and that they bring them as witnesses before the Committee to establish the charges of maltreating prisoners and of killing wounded.
>
> The Irgun Zvai Leumi in Eretz Israel[*]

UNSCOP chairman, Emil Sandström, cabled UN Secretary General Trygve Lie and persuaded him to express his concern about the death sentences to the British government. Behind closed doors, Whitehall was outraged at the UN's interference in the mandate's internal affairs. Officially, London responded by informing the UN head that the case was *sub judice* and could therefore not be discussed in public.

In the field, Irgun operatives continued in their attempts to abduct British military personnel to use as a bargaining tool, or to execute in the event of the hangings taking place. On 8 July, the administration confirmed the death sentences—the Irgun was running out of time to find hostages.

Then, on the evening of Saturday 12 July, as off-duty British sergeants of No. 552 Field Security Section, Intelligence Corps, Clifford Martin of Coventry and Mervyn Paice of Bristol, left the Café Gan Vered in Natanya, Irgun fighters drove up and bludgeoned and chloroformed the two surprised servicemen before trussing them and bundling them into the car.

When the two sergeants came to they had been carried into a cramped underground bunker beneath a deserted diamond factory in Natanya. Before sealing them into the airtight chamber—with two oxygen bottles and food and water for a week—the reason for their abduction was explained to them, including the outcome if their Irgun comrades were hanged.

Years of threat and counter-threat had reached a critical flashpoint as Revisionist Jew and the British Mandate authority confronted the other's uncompromising interpretation of justice. High Commissioner Alan Cunningham was not prepared to rescind his decision to execute the three Irgun fighters, a position that hardened considerably when the Royal Navy intercepted and sailed the Haganah refugee ship *Exodus 1947* into the port of Haifa on 18 July.

The former USS *President Warfield* was ferrying 4,500 Jewish survivors of the Holocaust from Europe. Members of UNSCOP saw for themselves the desperate, shocking conditions on board the packet steamer. Most of what the British regarded as illegal immigrants would be sent to camps in Cyprus. For a short while, the *Exodus* redirected the spotlight away from the Irgun death sentences conundrum.

---

[*] Begin.

An Eye for an Eye

Jewish immigrants on the *Exodus 1947*. (Photo Israel GPO)

At 4.03 a.m. on 29 July, Avshalom Haviv was hanged at Acre Prison. Meir Nakar was hanged at 4.28 a.m. and Yaakov Weiss at 5.02 a.m.

As news of the hangings filtered out, the following day Paglin hastened to Begin's safe house where the latter was already meeting with other members of the Irgun high command. There was a consensus that the presence of large numbers of very alert British troops would make transferring the two sergeants extremely risky, Paglin suggested that they be hanged in the building where they were being held. Begin and his fellow commanders agreed, and Paglin immediately set off in his car for Natanya. A statement had already been prepared for the underground newspaper, *Irgunpress*:

> We recognize no one-sided laws of war. If the British are determined that their way out of the country should be lined by an avenue of gallows and of weeping fathers, mothers, wives, and sweethearts, we shall see to it that in this there is no racial discrimination. The gallows will not all be of one colour ... Their price will be paid in full.*

---

* Bowyer Bell.

At the diamond factory a noose had been strung through a hook in the roof above a wooden chair. One at a time, the dazed sergeants were brought into the room, bound hand and foot, a hood placed over their heads, and hanged by having the chair knocked out from under their feet. After twenty minutes, the two bodies were brought down, before being transported to a copse of trees at Beit Lid, some three miles southeast of Natanya. Here the bodies were hanged from a eucalyptus tree and booby-trapped. When British troops arrived the next day to cut the bodies down, several were injured when the explosive devices were tripped.

Revulsion and anger swamped a stunned Britain. In Sergeant Martin's home town of Coventry, an editorial comment in the *Coventry Evening Telegraph* of 31 July accurately reflected the emotions and sentiments of the British public:

> [In] the lurid story of terrorism in Palestine no more brutal or callous act has been committed than the murder of Sergts. Clifford Martin and Mervyn Paice, of the British Intelligence Corps.
>
> The circumstances leading up to this cold-blooded crime which sullies the name of Palestine are such that it will horrify the civilised world. Chloroformed and kidnapped nearly three weeks ago by members of the terrorist organisation, Irgun Zvai Leumi, the men were spirited away, and continuous searching, in which the Haganah joined, has revealed no trace of them until their bodies were found this morning. They were held as hostages, and the British authorities in Palestine were threatened with their death if the execution of three terrorists sentenced for attempted gaol-breaking was carried out. The British did not yield to this intimidation, and the two men were murdered.
>
> The Irgun Zvai Leumi organisation have underlined with cruel emphasis their claim to be at war with the British in Palestine. It is a war in which no act is too foul for them to achieve their ends, a war in which they copy the barbarism of the Nazis, a war in which only one side fights. Against the ruthlessness of these terrorists the British must exercise restraint in fulfilling an onerous mandate to preserve the peace in Palestine.
>
> We cannot go on like this. Palestine is not worth the sacrifice of the lives of British boys and the murder of the two we mourn to-day ought to make insistent the demand that the United Nations relieves us of an impossible task without a day's unnecessary delay.

The loss of another three British constables in Palestine, when the bomb they were trying to remove from the Palestine Government Labour Department in Jerusalem on 5 August exploded, fuelled the vehemence on the streets of Britain that their nation's mandate in Palestine had to end as quickly as possible, that the UN should take over and resolve the situation.

6. ARMS NOT VOTES

> The Irgun Zvai Leumi, which rose up against the regime of British subjugation, smote it, brought about its disintegration, forced its armies of occupation to evacuate the country and thus made possible the sovereignty and independence of the People of Israel in their homeland.
>
> Having accomplished their task as an armed underground and as an independent military entity, within the present boundaries of the State of Israel, the officers and men of the Irgun Zvai Leumi vow not to rest and not to relax until the final aim to which they give their oath, is fulfilled—until the whole country is liberated from the yoke of foreign rule and returned to the people of Israel.
>
> Declaration of Irgun Zvai Leumi, 1948[*]

On 30 August, the much-anticipated UNSCOP report and its recommendations was made public: termination of the British Mandate and the partition of Palestine into independent Jewish and Arab states, linked by a customs union. While the news was welcomed by the Jewish Agency as the way forward, the Revisionists, including the Irgun and Lehi, were against partition.

The Revisionist Zionists dogmatically clung to Jabotinsky's vision of Eretz Yisrael—the land of Israel—the Promised Land bequeathed by God to the descendants of the Biblical patriarch, Abraham. This spiritual tract of real estate, delineated in the Hebrew 'Five Books of Moses', the Torah, was considerably larger than that of the twentieth-century British Mandate. For this right-wing movement, 'ownership' of Eretz Yisrael was literally their inviolable God-given birth right.

The British tenure of Palestine, originating as spoils of the First World War for ousting the Ottomans and secured by a vote in the League of Nations in June 1922, was regarded by the Revisionists as illegal. Twenty-five years later, a remodelled international body, the United Nations, voted in favour of Resolution 181 (II) "with regard to the future government of Palestine, of the Plan of Partition with Economic Union". Britain would relinquish its mandatory power over Palestine on 1 August 1948.

The Arab League rejected any suggestion of a Jewish state in *their* holy land. The Palestinian Arabs could no longer remain peacefully seated on the side-lines while Britain and the Jews fought each other over the fundamental issues for a lasting solution. War matériel was acquired and anti-Jewish violence recommenced.

---

[*] Tavin & Alexander.

Irgun: Revisionist Zionism 1931–1948

Menachem Begin, 1948.

On Saturday 29 November, the UN General Assembly approved the partition of Palestine into separate Jewish and Arab states. There were ten abstentions, including Britain. Euphoria erupted across the Jewish diaspora and among orthodox Jews in Palestine. But for the Irgun and like-minded Revisionists, a Jewish state without Jerusalem—the city would have 'international' status—was anathema.

For Begin this was not a victory and the Irgun rejected partition in its entirety:

> A tiny little state ... a mutilated Eretz Yisrael without Jerusalem and without Haifa, without land and without water, without freedom and without a future.

The eventual Zionist state would be limited only by the capacity of Zionist rifles. States were made with arms, not votes—against the British, against the Arabs, against anyone standing in the way of the future.*

The War of Independence had begun.

In the first twelve days following the UN vote for partition, more than a hundred people were killed in clashes between Jews and Arabs.

An Associated Press correspondent in Tel Aviv, quoted in the British newspaper *Northern Whig* on 3 December 1947, reported hearing machine-gun fire from "both sides of the dingy market place which divides the two cities of Jaffa and Tel Aviv". And in Jerusalem, "Rioting, stoning, burning and looting broke out [as] thousands of Arabs, armed with knives, stones and staves swept out of the old walled city to

---

* Bowyer Bell.

burn, loot and beat up Jews" in the modern section of the city. As the Palestine police quelled the riots, "angry Jews swarmed out of Zion Square and crashed through police barriers to begin the destruction of Arab shops, cinemas and cafés. The expression on the faces of Jews and Arabs alike ... were expressions of hate, fear and the lust for blood".

On 31 December, in the worst rioting in Palestine since the UN announced its plans for partition, forty-one Jews and six Arabs were killed at the Consolidated Oil Refineries plant near Haifa. A week later, the Irgun retaliated by dropping a 45-gallon drum of TNT and scrap metal in the Jaffa Gate square in Jerusalem. The explosion near the No. 3 bus stop killed seventeen Arabs and wounded over fifty.

The Arabs hit back on 1 February 1948, by detonating a pick-up truck packed with half a ton of TNT in front of the Palestine Post building, causing severe damage. Three weeks later, another car bomb exploded in Jerusalem, this time on Ben Yehuda Street, killing fifty-two people. On 11 March, a car bomb exploded opposite the Haganah headquarters in the courtyard of the Jewish Agency, killing thirteen and wounding more than forty.

As Arab acts of terror peaked in March, they now controlled the main inter-city routes, allowing for almost daily ambushes on vehicle convoys. Jewish settlements in the Negev and Galilee were left isolated, while the main arterial road into Jerusalem was blocked.

After weeks of intensive logistical and operational planning, the Haganah high command launched Operation Nachshon on 6 April, with the objective of opening the road to the beleaguered Jerusalem. Weaponry had been smuggled in by air and sea, and for the first time, the Haganah was able to field a brigade-sized force. Discovering that the Irgun and Lehi had already planned a raid on the village of Deir Yassin (population 600), the Haganah's Jerusalem commander, former French Foreign Legion sergeant, David Shaltiel, tried to persuade his Irgun and Lehi counterparts in Jerusalem, to once more join forces with the Haganah to execute the major operation. The Irgun commander, Mordechai Raanan, could not forget being kidnapped by the Haganah during its 'Hunting Season', resulting in an acrimonious verbal exchange and a failure by the Haganah to coax the Irgun back under their control.

At a pre-operational briefing, Raanan elaborated on the reasons for the attack on Deir Yassin. Whilst the immediate objective was the neutralization of Arab militant activities emanating from the village, once occupied it would be the jumping-off point for attacks into Arab territory. The prime objective was to take the fighting into the Arabs' backyard.

At 2 a.m. on 9 April, around seventy Irgun fighters, commanded by Ben-Zion 'Giora' Cohen, departed by truck from the Etz Hayim base at the entrance to Jerusalem. At Bet Hakerem, the force split up into smaller squads to take up predesignated

Boys unloading coils of barbed wire for the Haganah at Kibbutz Ein Harod, 1948. (Zoltan Kluger/ GPO Israel)

positions. The Lehi group had arrived at the Jewish village of Givat Shaul, from where an armoured car drove toward the village calling on the occupants to evacuate immediately.

Fighting commenced at 4.45 a.m., but heavy resistance from well-armed villagers immediately inflicted casualties on their Jewish assailants. The use of grenades deemed ineffective at clearing houses, Raanan brought forward rucksacks loaded with TNT for his men to use to blow up houses where strong resistance was being encountered. By 11 a.m., the village head's house, a stubborn stronghold during the fighting, fell to Irgun fighters, and with it the firing ceased.

The next day, the news agency Reuter covered the story following what they referred to as a "cloak and dagger" press conference by the Irgun and Lehi commanders. British correspondents, deemed "untrustworthy", had not been invited. From the press briefing, it was gleaned that 200 Arabs had been killed in the action, including a hundred women and children.*

---

* *Western Morning News*, 10 April 1948.

International Committee of the Red Cross representatives in Palestine, led by Jacques de Reynier, visited Deir Yassin on the 11th, where they reportedly saw the bodies of more than 200 Arab men, women and children. At the time of the visit, the Irgun gang was "wearing country uniforms with helmets". Conducting a "cleaning up" operation, de Reynier wrote that "All of them were young, some even adolescents, men and women, armed to the teeth: revolvers, machine-guns, hand grenades, and also cutlasses in their hands, most of them still blood-stained."*

As the news broke of what was now referred to as the Deir Yassin Massacre, casualty numbers, the circumstances of their deaths and the behaviour of Irgun fighters in the immediate aftermath varied considerably. The 'truth' of the events on that day is still being debated. Shaltiel, disassociating the Haganah from the tragedy, was unreserved in the Haganah's condemnation of the Irgun and Lehi, whose "soldiers stood and slaughtered men, women, and children, not in the course of the operation [Nachshon], but in a premeditated attack which had as its intention slaughter and murder only".†

As the British worked towards the target of 15 May for evacuation, the mandatory power continued to withdraw its forces from vulnerable areas, such as Tiberias, which the Haganah attacked and captured. Throughout the mandate, thousands of Arabs fled their homes. Following the withdrawal of the 6th Airborne, by the end of April an estimated 60,000 Arabs had left the port city of Haifa as Haganah forces took control.

During this period of Jewish ascendency in Palestine—the War of Independence—the Irgun found its ranks swelling with recruits caught up in the fervour of the prospect of a Zionist military victory that would deliver Eretz Yisrael.

Situated in what became the Tel Aviv-Yafo conurbation, in 1948 Jaffa, with a population of 90,000, was the largest Arab town in Palestine. Sharing a common boundary with Tel Aviv, since the announcement of partition, from which Jaffa was excluded, Arab snipers in Manshiya had made life for the neighbouring Jews extremely hazardous.

In what would be the largest Irgun operation to date, Begin and the high command selected Jaffa in which to neutralize the Arab threat to Israeli independence in the city. The accomplished mastermind of previous Irgun operations, the twenty-six-year-old Amichai 'Gigi' Paglin was appointed overall commander of what was dubbed Operation Hametz.

On 24 April, 600 Irgun fighters—other figures go as high as 3,000— mustered at Dov camp in Ramat Gan, a satellite town of Tel Aviv. Appearing publicly for

---

* David Hirst, *The Gun and the Olive Branch* (Faber and Faber, 1977).
† Bowyer Bell.

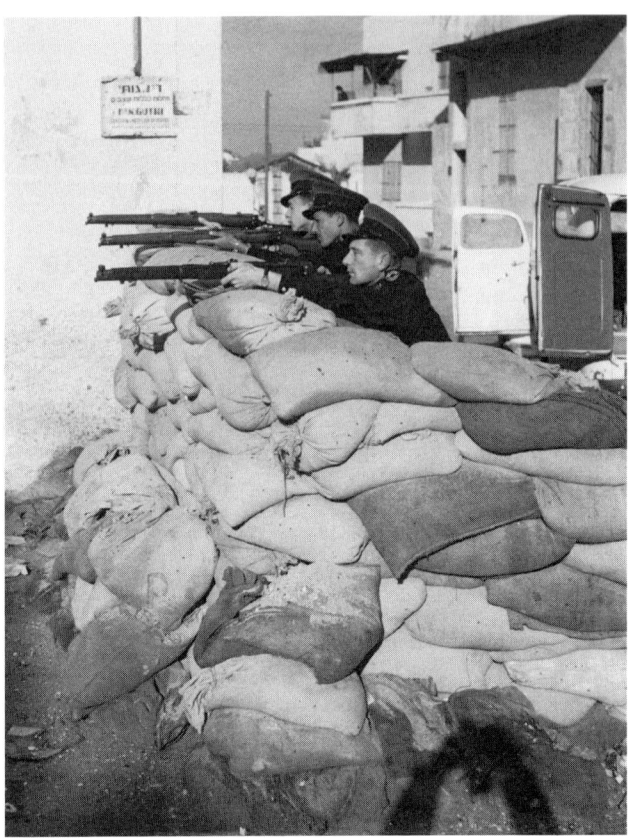

Tel Aviv policemen behind sandbags on the border with Jaffa, (Photo Israel GPO)

the first time since 'war' was declared, Begin addressed the parade of armed and equipped Irgun fighters:

> Soldiers of the Irgun!
> We are going to conquer Jaffa. We are setting out on one of the decisive battles in the struggle for Israel's independence.
> Know who stands before you, remember who you have left behind. You face a cruel foe, who wishes to destroy us. Behind you are our parents, our brethren, our children.
> Strike at the foe! Aim well! Spare ammunition! In this battle, show no mercy to the enemy, as he knows none towards our people. Spare women and children. Spare the life of anyone who raises his hands in surrender. He is your captive. Do not harm him.*

---

* www.etzel.org.il

At 3 a.m. on the morning of 25 April, a miscellany of borrowed, commandeered and pilfered trucks ferried the Irgun strike force along narrow, deserted Tel Aviv streets towards Jaffa. Tactical HQ was set up at the damaged Alliance School buildings and a field hospital established at the vacant Freud Hospital.

At dawn, the operation was launched as, hour after hour, the Irgun fired hundreds of bombs from only two 3-inch mortar tubes into Manshiya. However, for the first two days, strongly defended and protected Arab positions, many equipped with German MG42 'Spandau' machine guns, kept the Irgun out while inflicting increasing casualties in its ranks. There was also the realization that British tanks and armoured cars were bolstering the Arab stronghold.

On the third day of the assault, Paglin, accepting that frontal attacks were too exposed to Arab fire, changed his tactics. Advances would be through buildings which offered greater protection. Walls were breached by drilling or blasting and open areas barricaded with thousands of sandbags. In this manner, the Irgun strike force inched forward, eventually capturing the Manshiya police station. Arab resistance collapsed, allowing some Irgun units to reach the sea early the following morning.

With the Arab line in disarray, British tanks moved on Manshiya on the morning of 30 April. The British had given the mayor of Tel Aviv, Israel Rokach, an ultimatum to stop the Irgun from their attack, or face being shelled by tanks on land and bombardment from offshore British warships. Paglin ignored the warning, resulting in a British shelling of the Irgun HQ at the Alliance School. The commander responded with his own ultimatum: cease the bombardment, or mortar fire would be directed at the British garrison at the German Colony in Jaffa. The next British demand relayed through the Lydda district governor, called instead for only the return to them of the Manshiya police station and the handing over of the Irgun's positions to the Haganah. Treating the second demand with equal disdain, Paglin sent his engineers to blow up the police station, in addition to demolishing houses to block the road to Tel Aviv. Satisfied that his objectives had been successfully attained, Paglin relinquished their positions to Haganah forces. The Irgun had lost, depending on the source, between thirty and forty fighters during the operation. The Haganah deployed the highly effective Irgun mortars to continue fighting elsewhere. The British press reported that 80 percent of Jaffa's Arab population had fled.

On 12 May, Arab Jaffa capitulated, formally surrendering to the Haganah in Tel Aviv, heralding a quick succession of key events in the history of the Palestine Mandate. On the 14th, the Jewish National Council proclaimed the birth of the new Jewish State of Israel, "open to all Jewish immigrants". David Ben-Gurion would become the first prime minister. The next day, British High Commissioner Sir Alan Cunningham flew from Jerusalem to Haifa, where he boarded the cruiser HMS *Euryalous* for his final return trip to Britain—Palestine was no longer his concern.

Irgun: Revisionist Zionism 1931–1948

Lieutenant-General Sir Alan Cunningham at Lydda Airport on his arrival in Palestine in November 1945. (Photo Sergeant Meek)

With the final withdrawal of British troops on 15 May, the Irgun took over the just-vacated Generali Building in Jerusalem's heavily fortified 'Bevingrade' zone, followed by the former British intelligence HQ in the Russian Compound and the central prison. From there, elements of the Irgun seized the Police Academy, where they uncovered a large cache of ammunition and fuel. The Arab Quarter of Upper Sheikh Jarrah was next to fall to the Irgun, thereby reopening the road to Mount Scopus. Five days later, the Jordanian army—the Arab Legion—attacked Jerusalem, taking over the Police Academy and Sheikh Jarrah. At the same time, the Egyptian army invaded from the south toward Jerusalem, taking the Ramat Rachel kibbutz en route. After pushing the Egyptians out of the kibbutz, two Irgun platoons and a reinforced Haganah squad assumed defence duties of the settlement.

An Egyptian armoured column, comprising nine armoured cars and a tank, returned on 24 May. Remarkably, and without any anti-tank weapons, the Jewish fighters refused to yield. At last light, the Egyptians withdrew. The Jewish Agency feted the Irgun as having "displayed great heroism". A greater accolade came from Shaltiel, who stated that by repelling the Egyptians, the Irgun had saved southern Jerusalem.

Bitter fighting between Arab forces and the now amalgamated Haganah and Irgun continued well into June, when a four-week truce was agreed to. For the Irgun battalion of Jerusalem, this was a time for urgent consolidation, re-equipping and structural rationalization. Retitled Battalion 6, the unit was commanded by the thirty-two-year-old Nathan-Niko 'Shimshon' Germant, with Yehoshua 'Elitzur' Brandeis-Cohen as second-in-command. The battalion comprised three combat companies, a mortar company, a women's company and a youth company.

The ultimate demise of the Irgun as an independent Jewish fighting force commenced with the departure of the Irgun-owned ship, *Altalena*, from the French port of Sète. Captained by American Jew Monroe Fein, the cargo vessel was loaded with 2,000 rifles, two million rounds of ammunition, 3,000 shells and 200 Bren guns, a gift from the French government to the Irgun. Nearly 1,000 Irgun recruits were also on board, commanded by Revisionist Zionist activist Eliyahu Lankin. The *Altalena* dropped anchor off the coast at Kfar Vitkin late on 20 June. In Tel Aviv, Ben-Gurion would brook no compromise: Begin had to hand over the war matériel or be fired on.

While unloading the bulky cargo onto the beach, Paglin learned that IDF troops had surrounded their position, while three naval corvettes patrolled off the coast. The veteran Irgun commander wanted to load the arms back onto the *Altalena*, but Begin refused, electing instead to replace Paglin with Meridor. Late in the afternoon, the IDF

Smoke pours out of the *Altalena* after being shelled. (Photo Israel GPO)

troops opened fire, killing six and wounding eighteen Irgun fighters. Artillery was then ordered to shell the ship. The obdurate Begin was eventually forced off the ship by some of his colleagues, from where he went into hiding in Jaffa. The overall casualties during the *Altalena* incident amounted to sixteen Irgun fighters and three IDF soldiers.

The Haganah launched Operation Kedem on 14 July. After losing seventeen fighters in the attack on the Arab village of Malha, the Irgun was tasked with breaking through the Old City's New Gate, opposite Notre Dame, in a three-pronged Israeli attack to liberate Jerusalem. The fighters were successful, but the Beit Horon Battalion of the Israel Defence Forces (IDF) and Lehi failed to achieve their objectives, resulting in Shaltiel ordering his forces to withdraw and to cease fighting.

As this second truce drew to an end, western Jerusalem was in Jewish control, while the eastern section remained in Arab hands. At this time, Irgun commanders held successful negotiations with the provisional government for the Irgun to merge with the IDF. It was agreed that the Irgun in Jerusalem would be disbanded and its fighters given the option of enlisting in the IDF.

Following the assassination of UN Emissary Count Bernadotte at the hands of Lehi on 17 September, Lehi was proscribed and its bases raided by the IDF. As a direct consequence, three days later, the Irgun high command was issued with a twenty-four-hour ultimatum to lay down their arms and to enlist in the IDF. Failure to do so would result in army action "with all the means at its disposal". As the deadline approached, the Irgun acquiesced:

> In response to the ultimatum submitted to us yesterday, we hereby announce that, taking into consideration the threat of the use of force, and our desire to avoid shedding Jewish blood as a result of the execution of this threat, we accept the ultimatum. The Irgun Zvai Le'umi will disband in accordance with the Provisional Government's demands in a manner which will be determined between us and the commander of the IDF brigade in Jerusalem.[*]

Menachem Begin, co-founder and head of the Likud Party, became Israel's sixth prime minister in 1977. As Revisionist and head of the Irgun, he would never concede defeat; a much larger Eretz Yisrael was unsuccessfully fought for in a manner that shocked the world and orthodox Jews. But Begin was not an apologist for Irgun methodology, as he reveals in the closing sentences of his book *The Revolt*:

> If these chapters serve in any way to invoke that spirit [of freedom], and to deepen man's faith in his ability to smash his fetters—the author will be amply

---

[*] Ibid.

Memorial on Tel Aviv beach to the Irgun arms ship *Altalena*. (Photo Dr Avishai Teicher)

rewarded. But the author knows it was not he who will have earned this achievement. It is [my] duty therefore, to pay humble tribute to those whose achievement it is, to all who gave their lives for our people and for the renewal of our days of old.

I hope, however, that I may be permitted, at the close of these chapters, to pay my last and special tribute to the heroes and martyrs of the Irgun Zvai Leumi.

Their life was struggle; their death heroism; their sacrifice sacred; their memory eternal.

Sources

Allon, Yigal, *The Making of Israel's Army* (Valentine, Mitchell, London, 1970)

Begin, Menachem, *The Revolt: The Warrior Years of Israel's Brilliant Architect of Peace* (Dell Publishing, New York, 1977)

Bowyer Bell, J., *Terror Out of Zion: The Violent and Deadly Shock Troops of Israeli Independence 1929–1949* (St. Martin's Press, New York, 1977)

Hoffman, Bruce, *Anonymous Soldiers: The Struggle for Israel 1917–1947* (Vintage Books, New York, 2016)

Segev, Tom, *One Palestine, Complete: Jews and Arabs Under the British Mandate* (Abacus, London, 2014)

US Office of Strategic Services, *The Objectives and Activities of the Irgun Zvai Leumi* (October 1944)

von Pivka, Otto, *Armies of the Middle East* (Book Club Associates, London, 1979)

This photo, originally entitled 'Suddenly refugees forever', shows a girl and an old man in a Palestinian refugee camp, 1948. (Hanini)

Index

Abdullah, Emir
  (of Trans-Jordan) 26
Abramovitch, Aharon 94
Acre Prison 26, 44, 103, 106,
  107, 111
  breakout 86, 106, 107
Ajami, Nazim Ezra 88
al Kilani, Rashid Ali 67
Alexander II, Tsar,
  assassination of 16
al-Husayni, Hussein Bey 22
al-Husayni, Jamal 54
al-Husseini, Haj Amin 35, 39
Aliyah Bet 34, 35
Alkahi, Mordechai 100-104
Allenby, Gen Edmund 20-23,
  25, 26
Allison, Cst William 76
Altalena, shelling of 121, 122
Altman, Aryeh 64
Andrews, Lewis 39
Arab Higher Committee
  (AHC) 35-37, 39
Arab League 91, 107, 113
Arab Legion 120
Ariel, Shmuel 'Elhanan' 96
Arlosoroff, Chaim (Victor)
  32, 33
Arlosoroff, Sima 33
Ashbel, Michael 88, 89, 96
Assault Force (AF) 73-75
Atlee, Clement 84, 91
Avni, Yosef 94

Baghdad 67
  Railway 19
Balfour, Arthur James 22-24
  Declaration 20, 22, 25
Barazani, Moshe 97, 105
Barker, Gen Evelyn 99, 101-103
Barker, Insp Ronald 61
Barnes, Cst Stanley 105
Beersheba 21, 22
Begin, Herzl 69
Begin, Menachem 13, 53, 68-70,
  72, 73, 81, 84, 85, 98, 111, 114,
  117, 118, 121-123

Ben-Eliezer, Aryeh 69
Ben-Gaon, David 43
Ben-Gurion, David 18, 32, 33,
  54, 55, 83, 94, 103, 119
Ben-Shem, Avner 89
Ben-Yosef, Shlomo 43-45
Benziman, Asher (Avshalom) 75
Berman, Yitzhak 67
Bernadotte, Count 122
Betar 27, 30, 34, 35, 39, 43, 53,
  66, 68-72
Bethlehem 21, 8, 59, 76
Bet-Zuri, Eliyahu 82
Bevin, Ernest 84, 85, 91
Birnbaum, Nathan 18
Bitker, Col Robert 39
Brandeis-Cohen, Yehoshua
  'Elitzur' 121
Brett, Maj Paddy 99
Brown, Cst Charles 76

Cairo 37, 48, 49, 67, 82, 105
Cairs, Insp Ralph 61
Caley, Cst Douglas 76
Casey, Cst Alan 105
Cassels, Gen James 90, 91
Chamberlain, Neville 53,
  62, 63
Churchill, Winston 11, 25, 82,
  83, 103
Clark, Cst Robert 59
Cohen, Dov 'Shimshon'
  87, 89, 107
Cohen, Rahamim 75
Collins, Maj H. A. I. 101
Criminal Investigation
  Department (CID) 65, 66,
  75, 76, 81, 85, 86
Cunningham, Gen Alan 101,
  102, 110, 119, 120
Curzon, George 25

Davies, Cst Ronald 105
de Reynier, Jacques 117
Deedes, Gen Wyndham 28
Deir Yassin, massacre at
  115-117

Dill, Gen John 36
Dov camp 117
Drezner, Yehiel 101-104

Egyptian Expeditionary Force
  19, 20
Eliav, Yaakov 85
Exodus refugee stand-off
  110, 111

Fein, Monroe 121
Feinstein, Meir 97, 105
Flanagan, Asst Supt F. 86
Frankel, Zvi 39
Friedlander, Magda
  (Frau Goebbels) 33

Galili, Yisrael 85
Gaza 21, 22
General Organization of
  Workers (Histadrut) 27, 49
Georges-Picot, François 22
Germant, Nathan-Niko
  'Shimshon' 121
Giles, Arthur 65
Gillam, Sgt Terence 99
Goebbels, Joseph 33
Golomb, Eliyahu 50, 81
Golovsky, Haim 'Gilad'
  100, 101
Great Arab Revolt 20
Gromyko, Andrei 107, 108
Gruner, Dov 101-104

Haganah 13, 25, 27, 29, 31, 36,
  47, 50, 82, 83, 85, 89, 90, 92,
  94, 110, 115-117, 119-121
Haichman, Aaron 39
Haifa 31, 39, 42, 43, 49, 55, 59,
  60, 61, 75, 77, 85, 106, 110, 114
Hakim, Eliyahu 82
Harazi, Yaakov 67
Harding, Cst Arthur 76
HaShomer HaTzair
  (The Young Guard) 80
Haviv, Avshalom 107-109, 111
Haycraft, Thomas 26

Hays, J. L. 89
Hebrew Committee of National Liberation (HCNL) 80
Hebron 21, 22, 28, 45, 47
Hedjaz railway 19
Heichman, Ahron 63
Herzl, Theodor 16-18, 26
Herzog, Rabbi 44
Hess, Rudolf 51
HMS *Emerald* 48
HMS *Euryalous* 119
HMS *Repulse* 48, 49
Holocaust 11, 64, 67, 69, 84, 110
Hyde, Cst 86

Intelligence Corps 110, 112
Irish Republican Army (IRA) 61
Israeli Defence Forces (IDF) 13, 121, 122

Jabotinsky, Ari 35
Jabotinsky, Ze'ev 11, 25-27, 31, 32, 34-36, 39, 40, 53, 57, 66-68, 72, 113
Jaffa 22, 26, 47, 48, 75, 77, 85, 98, 114, 117, 118
Jerusalem 21, 22, 25, 28, 31, 34, 35, 38, 44-50, 54, 55, 58, 60, 61, 73, 74, 76, 85, 86, 97, 114, 115, 120-122
   Old City of 28, 31, 44, 46, 49, 50, 54, 55, 93
Jewish Agency 13, 27, 31, 32, 36, 42, 54, 81, 83, 85, 89, 91, 92, 94, 95, 115, 120
Jewish Brigade 13
Jewish Labour Party 49
Jewish Legion 26
Jewish National Assembly of Palestine 65
Jewish National Council (in Palestine) 103
Jewish Self-Defence Organization (Russia) 26

Kalai (Strelitz), Hanoch 57, 58, 63
Kalay, Charnoch 39
Kashani, Eliezer 100-104

Katz, Samuel 96
Keith-Roach, Edward 45
Kfar Saba 100
Kfar Sirkin airfield (RAF Petah Tikva), raid on 86, 87
Kimchi, Benjamin
King David Hotel 11, 13, 65, 38, 84, 92, 93
   bombing of 11, 84, 86, 92-97
King, Sgt Geoffrey 61
Kol Tsion HaLokhemet (Voice of Fighting Zion) 80
Kook, Hillel 30

Labour Zionists *see* Zionist Workers' Party
Lankin, Eliyahu 68, 69, 121
Latrun camp 92
Lawrence, T. E. 20
League of Nations 25, 46, 113
Lehi (Lohamei Herut Yisrael) 30, 44, 59, 66, 81, 82, 85-87, 89, 90, 93, 95, 104, 106, 113, 115-118, 122
Lemberger, Jehuda 63
Lev-Ami, Shlomo (Levi) 69
Levi, Yisrael 'Gidon' 94
Lie, Trygve 110
Lifshitz, Zalman 106
Likud Party 122
Livni, Eitan 85, 89, 106
Lloyd George, David 22, 23
London Conference 55
Lydda 85, 98
   airfield, raid on 87

MacDonald, Malcolm 53-55
Mackie, Cst James 76
Mandate, British (of Palestine) 11, 13, 25, 26, 28, 31, 36, 37, 41, 45, 46, 50, 54, 57, 75, 82, 83, 95, 98, 101-103, 110, 113, 119
Martin, Sgt Clifford 110-112
McMahon–Hussein Correspondence 20
Meridor, Yaakov 53, 64, 67-69, 73, 121
Michaeli, Amnon 107

Mizrachi Party 30
Mizrahim Avraham 100
Mount of Olives 21
Moyne, Lord (Walter Guinness) 82
Murray, Gen Archibald 19, 20
MV *Sinbad II* 61

Nakar, Meir 107-109, 111
Nashashibi, Fakhri Bey 45
National Military Organization (Irgun Zvai Leumi) 30
Nazareth 39, 48
Netanya 99, 100, 110
New Zionist Organization (NZO) 34-39, 53, 54, 64
Nicholson, Cst 86

O'Connor, Gen R. N. 45
Occupied Enemy Territory Administration (OETA) 24
Odessa Group (of Haganah) 29
Office of Strategic Services (OSS) 11
Ohevet-Ami (Habshush), Rachel 58, 59
Operatiom Elephant 102
Operation Chick 92
Operation Hametz 117-119
Operation Hippo 102
Operation Kedem 122
Operation Nachshon 115
Operation Polly 101
OSS *see* Office of Strategic Services
Ostrowicz, Menahem 107
Ottoman Empire *also* Ottomans 16, 19, 21, 22, 26, 47, 113

Paget, Gen Bernard 78
Paglin, Amichai 'Gidi' 86, 93, 106, 111, 117-119, 121
Palestine Broadcasting Service 77
Palmach (Plugot Hamahatz) *see also* Haganah 83, 85
Passfield, Lord (Sidney Webb) 31

Index

Peel, Robert 36, 38, 54
   Commission 36, 39, 54
Perelson, Acting Mayor 90, 91
Plaice, Sgt Mervyn 110-112
pogroms 16
Posek, Aryeh 67

Qastina airfield (RAF), raid on 87, 88

Raanan, Mordechai 115, 116
Rabia, Ezra 89
Rafia camp 91, 92
Ramallah 77
Ramele 36
Ramla 88
Ratner, Yohanan 29
Raz, Yaakov 49, 50
Raziel, David 30, 39, 40, 46, 53, 57, 63-66, 75
Red Cross, International Committee of the 117
Reinhold, Heinrich 'Yanai' 97
Revisionist Party 65, 71, 83, 89
Revisionist Zionism /Zionists *see also* New Zionist Organization (NZO) 11, 27, 30-37, 39, 42, 43, 53, 59, 65, 66, 68-70, 83, 110, 113, 114, 121, 122
Revolutionary Propaganda Force (RPF) 73, 83, 98-100
Rishon LeZion 99, 100
River Jordan 26, 27
Rokach, Israel 119
Rosenberg, Moshe 39
Rosenthal, David 47
Rosh Pina 43
Rothschild, James de 23
RPF *see* Revolutionary Propaganda Force
Rutenberg, Pinhas 65

Sadeh, Yitzhak 85
Salomon, Dov 'Yishai' 102, 106
Samuel, Herbert 24, 25
Sandström, Emil 110
Sarafand al Amar camp 63
   raid on 88
Sarona camp 84
Schiff, Menachem 'Zeev' 14, 89
Scott, Asst Supt John 76
Segal, Moshe Halevi 31
Serona police camp, attack on 105
Shai (Sherut Yediot) *see also* Haganah 83
Shaltiel, David 115
Shamir, Yitzhak 81, 82
Sharif of Mecca 20
Sharp, L/Cpl 86
Shaw, J. V. W. 78
Shein, Avraham 43
Sika-Aharoni, Yaakov 67
Simchon, Yosef 88, 89, 96
Smith, Cst G. F. 86
Sneh, Moshe 81, 85, 92
Stanley, Col 79
Stern Gang *see also* Lehi 45, 66, 68
Stern, Avraham 30, 39, 40, 53, 63, 65, 66, 68, 81
Sternglass, Dov 86
Sykes, Mark 22

Tamler, Eliyahu 88
Tavin, Ely 'Pesach' 96
Tavin, Yaakov (Farshtei) 83
Tehomi, Avraham 29, 30, 36, 39
Tel Aviv 18, 31-33, 36, 39, 42, 44, 47, 53, 55, 59, 63, 65, 67, 75, 77, 81, 84, 86, 89, 92, 99, 100, 114, 117-119, 121
   hotel abductions 89

Thompson, Downing 94
Truman, Harry S. 91
Trumpeldor, Joseph 25
Trutwein, Insp Allen 105
Turton, Evelyn Thomas 45

Union of Revisionist Zionists 27
United Nations 81, 103, 105-108, 110, 112-115, 122
   Special Committee on Palestine (UNSCOP) 105, 108, 110, 113
United Palestine Appeal 13
United Resistance 85, 86, 89, 92, 95

Wailing Wall 15, 31, 73-75
Weiss, Yaakov 107-109, 111
Weissenberg, May 61
Weizmann, Chaim Azriel 22, 40, 54, 92
White papers (British) 11, 25, 31, 54-57, 63, 70, 84, 85
Windham, Ralph 102
Wingate, Orde 50
Wolffsohn, David 18
World Zionist Organization (WZO) 18, 92

X Committee 92, 93

Yellin-Mor, Nathan 85
Yitzhaki, Gundar 'Arieh' 61

Zeroni, Benyamin 63, 64
Zionist Workers' Party 32, 33
Zionist world congresses 18, 28, 31, 41
Zurabin, Yehoshua (Shalom) 43

About the Author

Born in Southern Rhodesia, now Zimbabwe, historian and author Gerry van Tonder came to Britain in 1999. Specializing in military history, Gerry started his writing career with titles about twentieth-century guerrilla and open warfare in southern Africa, including the co-authored definitive Rhodesia Regiment 1899–1981. Gerry presented a copy of this title to the regiment's former colonel-in-chief, Her Majesty the Queen. Having written over twenty books, Gerry writes extensively for several Pen & Sword military history series including 'Cold War 1945–1991', 'Military Legacy' (focusing on the heritage of British cities), 'Echoes of the Blitz', and 'History of Terror'.

Other Titles by the Author

SS Einsatzgruppen: Nazi Death Squads 1939–1945
Sino-Indian War: October–November 1962
Echoes of the Coventry Blitz
Red China: Mao Crushes Chiang's Kuomintang, 1949
North Korea Invades the South: Across the 38th Parallel, June 1950
North Korean Onslaught: UN Stand at the Pusan Perimeter, August–September 1950
Berlin Blockade: Soviet Chokehold and the Great Allied Airlift 1948–1949
Malayan Emergency: Triumph of the Running Dogs 1948–1960
Nottingham's Military Legacy
Sheffield's Military Legacy
Derby in 50 Buildings
Chesterfield's Military Heritage
Mansfield Through Time
Rhodesian African Rifles/Rhodesia Native Regiment Book of Remembrance
Lt-Gen Keith Coster: A Life in Uniform
Rhodesian Combined Forces Roll of Honour 1966–1981
Rhodesia Regiment 1899–1981
Operation Lighthouse: Intaf in the Rhodesian Bush War 1972–1980 (2019)
North of the Red Line: Recollections of the Border War by Members of the South African Armed Forces: 1966–1989